How to cope after relationship abuse for men

Janet Haines
Mandy Matthewson

Acknowledgements:
Steven Haines
Robyn Cartledge
Coverart designed by Freepik
(www.freepik.com)

This workbook offers suggestions on how to cope in the aftermath of an abusive relationship. We do not guarantee that these suggested strategies will resolve all psychological symptoms. You may wish to seek alternative assistance from a mental health professional.

How to cope after relationship abuse for men
Janet Haines & Mandy Matthewson
Copyright © 2025
ISBN: 978-1-923573-11-6

About the authors

Dr Janet Haines has a PhD in Clinical Psychology and has worked as an academic and researcher for 17 years, and in private practice for 30 years helping people facing life problems.

Dr Mandy Matthewson is a Clinical Psychologist, educator and researcher with more than two decades of experience supporting people through life's toughest challenges.

For the men we have met who suffered for so long in silence but then spoke up.
And especially for those who did for their children
what they found hard to do for themselves.

Table of contents

Introduction 8
What the statistics tell you 9
The greatest myths of abuse 11
The nature of abuse 13
    Physical assault 13
    Sexual abuse 14
    Threats and intimidation/bullying 15
    Coercion 16
    Verbal abuse 17
    Humiliation 18
    Social isolation 19
    Abduction/deprivation of liberty 20
    Stalking 21
    Economic/financial abuse 22
The cycle of abuse 25
    The four stages of the abuse cycle 25
    What is the impact of this cycle of abuse? 25
Why did I stay? 27
    A complicated issue 27
    I was too scared to leave 27
    She said she would kill herself if I left 28
    But I loved her… 29
    The abuser's expressions of regret and promises of change 30
    There were children involved 31
    Loss of sense of self-efficacy and self-confidence 32
    Low sense of self-worth 32
    Lack of social support 33
The issue of gaslighting 35
    Types of gaslighting 35
    What should I be looking for? 38
    Indicators of gaslighting and the effects on you 44
My reaction to the end of the relationship 46
    The abuser ended the relationship 46
    You ended the relationship 46
    Grief and disenfranchised grief 46

What do I need to do now?	50
Keep yourself safe	52
Manage your anxiety/trauma	55
What is your nervous system doing?	55
Range of arousal	57
Anxiety management strategies	59
Quietening your mind	66
Dealing with sleep disturbance	72
What can I do about my sleep problems?	74
Regulating your emotions	76
Recognising and dealing with your emotions	77
The link between your emotions and your behaviour	81
Learn to cope	84
Problem-focused coping vs. emotion-focused coping	84
Problem-approach vs. problem-avoidance coping	85
Identifying your preferred coping style	87
Building your coping repertoire	91
Fix your thinking	102
How are our thoughts affected?	102
Core beliefs	103
Cognitive errors	103
Why do we think in unhelpful ways?	114
Underlying assumptions of logical errors	116
Understanding automatic thoughts	119
Catching automatic thoughts	119
Understanding and noticing logical errors	122
Reframing your thoughts (cognitive restructuring)	124
Making the restructured thinking habitual	128
Targeting the assumptions	128
Re-establish a sense of self and self-worth	132
Factors that enhance a sense of self and self-worth	132
How to build self-worth	133
Thoughts and beliefs to promote high self-worth	134
Re-build your self-efficacy	136
The concept of self-efficacy	136
The link between self-efficacy and relationship abuse	136
Why is self-efficacy important?	136

  Ways to improve self-efficacy 137
Understand your rights 143
Learn to be assertive 147
  Asking for change 147
  Negotiating for what you want 150
Improving the quality of your life 152
  Values clarification exercise for choosing preferred activities 152
Some final points 155
Additional readings 157

Introduction

This workbook has been written to help you cope with the recovery period after the end of an abusive relationship where you have been the target of your partner's abuse. We have focused on that time after the end of the relationship and not during the relationship for a couple of reasons.

Firstly, it is often the case that during an abusive relationship, you are in what we would label survival mode. You put one foot in front of the other to get through the day, and you have little time or headspace to consider your situation, how you are feeling and what to do. It is like being in an almost permanent crisis state. When you are focusing on handling a crisis, you do not have the capacity to care for your longer-term needs, including your mental health needs. You just try to hold things together because you have no choice but to do so.

Secondly, it is damaging to you to be in an abusive relationship. This is true from both a physical and psychological point of view. It is not easy to deal with that damage while the harm is still occurring. After the end of the relationship, your recovery needs that will promote your well-being can receive some attention without the interference of ongoing abuse.

In this workbook, the focus is on the recovery from the abuse and the damage it has caused you. However, it may be useful to consider the self-help options available to you at a time when you are considering leaving.

In this workbook, we are going to go over some aspects of abuse in a relationship because it is important for you to understand the nature of the influences on you and the ways you have been affected. Then, we will focus on the things you can do to help yourself in your recovery from the abusive relationship.

It is not the purpose of this workbook to replace the need for a therapeutic relationship with a psychologist or counsellor who can help you through this recovery process. It is designed to offer you ways to help yourself and to encourage you to see that recovery is possible.

What the statistics tell you

Undoubtedly, most of the information you see or hear about in the media relates to female victims of relationship violence. It gives the impression that being a male victim of female-perpetrated family violence is rare. That is not the case. To put your experience into a better perspective, we thought it was important to relay to you some of the statistics about male victims. This information is taken from the Australian Bureau of Statistics. This information was collected in 2016.

For your information:

> Just over 35% of people who experienced intimate partner violence were male. That is, more than one-third of victims of domestic abuse are male.

> About 33% of people who experienced violence from a partner with whom they cohabited were male.

> Almost 40% of people who experienced violence from a current partner were male.

> About 46% of people who experienced emotional abuse by a partner were male.

> Of the men who had been emotionally abused by their current partner, almost 14% (compared with 6% of females) had been deprived by their partner of basic needs such as food, shelter, sleep or assistive aids.

> Of the men who had been emotionally abused by their current partner, almost 9% (compared with 5% of women) had experienced their partner threatening to take their children away from them.

> Of the men who had been emotionally abused by their current partner, 38% (compared with 25% of women) had their partner tell their children untruths about them in an effort to turn the children against them.

> About 28% of people who had been sexually assaulted were men, with the majority (83%) having been sexually assaulted or sexually threatened by females.

> The vast majority of men who experienced intimate partner violence (94%) were the victims of a female perpetrator, with the others experiencing violence in same-sex relationships.

Despite these statistics, the following information should be noted:

> Men were identified to be 2-3 times more likely than women to have never disclosed to anyone about their experience of intimate partner violence.

> Men were found to be 50% more likely than women to have never sought help, advice or support in relation to experiencing intimate partner violence.

> Men were shown to be about 20% more likely than women to have never contacted the police about the intimate partner violence they were experiencing.

> Men were less than half as likely as women to have a restraining order issued in their favour in relation to intimate partner violence.

As you can see from these statistics, a significant proportion of all victims of intimate partner violence are men. Despite men experiencing this type of violence, they are significantly less likely to seek or receive help. So, why are people's views about men being victims of relationship violence so distorted?

The greatest myths of abuse

It is evident that there are a number of myths or erroneous beliefs about men being victims of relationship violence that have become established in the mentality of the general public. Let's consider some of these here.

Myth #1 - Society tells us that men are not victims of relationship abuse.

This is obviously incorrect. The statistics make it clear that men are victims of relationship abuse. Nevertheless, this generally held view discourages men from speaking out and seeking help. Further, even when they do, their reports can be dismissed. Assumptions can be made that male victims are the perpetrators. The fact is that men can and do experience violence from their intimate partners.

Myth #2 - The media portrays men as the perpetrators of relationship violence and women as the victims, but almost never the reverse, leading people to hold the view that men are always the perpetrators and never the victims.

To a significant degree, we have become desensitised to the notion of relationship violence because of the normalisation of this type of violence in the media. We are exposed to it often enough that we are not as shocked by it as we might have been in the past. We know that we can be influenced by what we learn from the media, so it is not surprising that we have come to accept that men are seen as perpetrators of abuse and not victims because of the constant exposure to this message. Of course, the fact that relationship violence is portrayed in this way in the media does not make it true.

Myth #3 - Men are not the victims of relationship violence when they are physically larger than their female partners.

It is a commonly held but incorrect belief that it is not possible for a male to be the victim of physical violence in a relationship if the man's partner is smaller in stature than the man. However, there are numerous factors that impact the perpetration of intimate partner violence that have no relationship to relative physical size. For example, a man may choose not to engage in violent behaviour, no matter the provocation from a volatile partner. Alternatively, a man may have a more passive temperament relative to his partner's more aggressive one. Also, a man may be overwhelmed by his violent partner's need to exert control. Of course, a man may be perceived as the aggressor because, superficially, they appear more imposing and physically more intimidating.

Myth #4 - A man is not a 'real man' if they cannot take what their partner doles out.

Stereotypical views of masculinity can cause men to contain their normal emotional reactions to the point that they are not expressed, even in situations that would be considered to warrant a strong emotional response. As a result of the belief that they should not demonstrate what they perceive as any weakness, men will not report abuse and will hold the view that it is shameful to disclose to others what is happening to them. Indeed, some male victims of relationship violence will not even admit to themselves that this is what they are experiencing.

None of these views have merit, but they do influence the way in which male victims of relationship violence are perceived and how likely they are to seek help. It is the case that men can be abused in the same or similar ways as women.

The nature of abuse

Here, we are going to consider different ways in which abuse manifests in a relationship and the ways in which each type of abuse can affect you. It is worth pointing out that there are other ways abuse in a relationship can present itself, and you can probably identify some of those other forms of abuse from your own experiences. An important point is that each separate type of abuse does not necessarily have a different effect on you. There are some commonalities in the challenges that the various forms of abuse can cause.

Physical assault

What is it?

By using the term assault, we are referring to any form of physical attack, whether or not it causes physical injury. In this way, assault ranges from behaviours such as pushing and shoving up to physical assault that causes grievous bodily harm that can result in life-changing and life-threatening injuries.

Whether or not medical assistance is sought in the aftermath of a physical assault cannot be used as a reliable indicator of the seriousness of the assault. Some people do not seek medical help for the injuries they sustain. This may be due to not wishing to be questioned about how the injuries occurred or the perpetrator of the abuse preventing the injured person from seeking medical attention. We have met people who have had bones broken as a result of relationship abuse but have not sought medical help or have been prevented from having their broken bones set.

It is not unusual for people who do seek medical attention for injuries caused by physical assault in a relationship to give an incorrect account of the cause of the injury to medical personnel. This is not about, or not only about, protecting the perpetrator of the abuse. It is more likely about protecting themselves from the reaction of the abuser to their disclosure to medical personnel about the true nature of the abuse.

> *Michael described the nature of the physical abuse he experienced. He said it would occur when his partner would become enraged and blame him for things that either hadn't happened or were not his fault. If she felt bad for any reason, Michael suffered. He gave an account of being dragged down the passage in his house by his hair. He said fists full of hair were pulled from his scalp, leaving wounds. He said she would unexpectedly punch him in the head, including while he was driving the car. He said she had slashed him with a knife. Michael said it was not in his nature to retaliate, and he was too frightened of her to do so in any case.*

How does it affect you?

By living in an environment where you can be physically attacked and harmed at any time, that environment becomes unsafe and unpredictable. This causes you to be in a permanent state of hypervigilance where you are on the lookout for signs that physical harm is imminent. So, you come to be in a permanent state of nervous system arousal. You become very sensitive to any signs of threat and experience a constant state of anxiety.

You also end up existing in a constant state of conflict between protecting the abuser and your relationship and protecting yourself. If you choose to protect yourself, you end up causing problems for the perpetrator and, potentially, damaging the relationship on which you have become dependent. Often, it is the perpetrator and the unhealthy relationship that comes out on top in this conflict. With your needs always being given the least consideration, you can come to value yourself as less important than the abuser or the maintenance of the relationship.

Sexual abuse

What is it?

Part of the experience of sexual abuse is sexual attack, that is, forced sexual intercourse that in this, as in other contexts, is considered to be rape. The fact that it takes place within an existing relationship does not change the nature of this type of attack. Without consent, the sexual intercourse is still forced and unwanted.

Some people may question whether males can be raped by a female, mistakenly assuming that a male must consent to intercourse. However, forced sexual activity does occur and has the same characteristics as any other act of rape.

As well as this type of assault, sexual abuse can be experienced in other forms that are still abusive in nature. For example, sexual abuse can involve you being coerced into engaging in sexual behaviour that is unwanted by you or that is degrading to you. You might agree to engage in the behaviour to please your partner or because you have been encouraged by the abuser to believe you have an obligation to do this, but if you were given a genuine choice, it is not what you would have chosen to do.

Another problem that can arise is the way in which an abusive partner can use sexual activity. For example, sexual behaviour can be used as a form of punishment by the abuser, either by withholding sexual intimacy or forcing unwanted sexual activity in response to a perceived wrongdoing on your part. The use of sexual activity in this way by the abuser does not rely on you having done anything wrong, only that the abuser believes you deserve punishment.

Another way in which sexual interactions with the abuser can be used by the abuser is through linking it with other negative interactions, such as a physical attack. For example, a severe episode of physical abuse can be followed by an aggressive sexual interaction, even in cases where you were physically injured and in pain.

> *Grant was referred to a psychologist by his general practitioner for assistance with sexual dysfunction. Grant was experiencing a combination of erectile dysfunction and premature ejaculation. He was in a new relationship with a supportive partner, and these problems were significant for Grant. He gave a history of an abusive relationship. He said he was the victim of his then-partner's violent behaviour and sexual demands. He said she would assault him, become overly aroused during the process and then force him to engage in sexual intercourse that was unwanted and confusing for him. He said those episodes had been distressing for him. Grant reported that sexual activity had become associated in his mind with distressing physical violence. He said he would become anxious when trying to be intimate with his new partner, who he described as a loving and caring person.*

How does this affect you?

Having your physical and psychological integrity threatened in a sexual way is a personal violation that can be quite intolerable for most people and can be traumatic in nature. It denies you the ability to have control over what is happening to you. In general, having little control in your life is anxiety-provoking and damages your sense of self and who you are.

Such treatment of you can cause you to become confused about the nature of relationships and distorts your views about the distinction between love and abuse. Loving feelings should not be expressed in ways that are harmful to you so it is not surprising that a deep sense of uncertainty about your worthiness as a person who is lovable develops.

Threats and intimidation/bullying

What is it?

Physical attacks and unwanted sexual activity are not necessary components of abuse. It is an emotionally abusive act to threaten such behaviour. This threat might be in the form of direct physical harm, such as a threat to break your arm or punch you in the face. However, the threat may also be indirect, with a suggestion of harm. An example would be that you will "get what is coming to you". There is no direct statement of what will happen, but you know that it will be bad.

The threats may not only be directed towards you. In an effort to indirectly threaten you and force you to do what the abuser wants, the abuser may threaten others who are important to you. This may be done directly (e.g., "I will beat up your sister") or indirectly (e.g., "Your sister will have to spend the rest of her life looking over her shoulder").

Threats and other forms of intimidation and bullying are aimed at controlling your behaviour. They encourage you to become and remain compliant in relation to the wishes of the abuser. The goal is to get you to do something you would otherwise not choose to do if you had not been threatened, intimidated or bullied.

> *Michael's partner threatened him repeatedly. She threatened to call the police and have him charged with assaulting her even though he had never done so and she had assaulted him. She threatened to place humiliating information about him on social media. She threatened to call his boss at work and claim she was the victim of relationship abuse. She threatened to tell his sick mother terrible things about him that were not true. Michael lived in fear of her following through with these threats. Whenever she threatened him, Michael would back down from any discussion. He felt he could not risk her doing any of these things.*

How does this affect you?

In the same way that an actual physical attack can cause you to be threat-sensitive and in a constant state of fear, to some degree, so does the threat of harm. You live in a state of alertness, looking for signs that the threat of harm is going to change to actual harm.

Further, when the threat is directed towards others you care about, you can take on board a sense of responsibility for the wellbeing of these people that is beyond what is reasonable. Given that you have very little control over what the abuser chooses to do, you end up worrying about things that you cannot influence. You keep trying to adjust your own behaviour to protect others despite the fact that there is no real way of doing so.

Coercion

What is this?

Abusive partners will use emotional manipulation to get you to do things you would otherwise not choose to do. Coercion can also be used to get you to abandon issues you would much prefer to confront, but the abuser does not want to be raised.

Abusers tend to focus on your greatest fears and vulnerabilities when coercing you into doing what they want. They take advantage of your emotional state, which has already been affected by other abusive experiences. You will feel like you have no choice but to do what they expect. It is like being put in an impossible situation that you cannot win.

> *Whenever Matthew tried to raise with his partner an issue about their relationship or her behaviour, she would threaten to kill herself. She made it clear that she would make sure that everyone knew that she had taken her own life because of him. She told him that their children would grow up knowing that their father had killed their mother. Her threats were dramatic, and she would say things about him that were denigrating and nasty. Matthew always backed down. He didn't know what else to do. As soon as he backed down, his partner would become sulky, dragging out her reaction for maximum effect. Then things would return to normal. Matthew became so sensitised to these episodes that he was fearful about raising any issue with his partner for fear it would trigger another round of threats.*

How does this affect you?

This type of coercion and emotional manipulation is psychologically damaging. It causes you to feel intense anxiety. It can make you feel helpless (i.e., there is nothing you can do to change things) and hopeless about the future (i.e., nothing is ever going to change). Feelings of helplessness and hopelessness are linked to feelings of depressed mood.

The use of coercion and emotional manipulation can strengthen the power imbalance in the relationship that is already in favour of the abuser. This type of power imbalance results in you feeling like you have little control over what happens to you and never feeling like your concerns are listened to or your needs met. It creates feelings of worthlessness and lack of value.

Verbal abuse

What is this?

Verbal abuse refers to a stream of belittling and demeaning rants directed at you by the abusive partner. This abuse may take the form of shouting but also may be quietly spoken. Its main characteristic is its unrelenting nature. Once triggered, the verbal abuse can persist for extended periods, wearing you down until you give in or shut down.

It is important to know that this type of abuse typically is not triggered by any wrongdoing on your part or, at least, not of sufficient severity that it would warrant this abuse. More likely, verbal abuse by the abuser is related to the abuser's personal characteristics, their behaviour or their displeasure based on their own interpretation of what is happening at that time.

> *Colin said he couldn't describe how bad it was when his partner started verbally abusing him. He said he could be just going about his normal business, and she would attack him. She would say things to him that were hateful and hurtful. She would say nasty things about his physical appearance, his intelligence, and his value as a man. He said that once she started, nothing could really stop her until she ran out of steam. He said the worst times were when she verbally attacked him when they were in public or with friends or family. He said if anyone tried to stand up to her, she just increased her attack on him. He said there was nothing he could do to stop her. He said it was better to just let her go and take it until she finished. However, there would always be a next time. It could happen at any time and in any circumstance. Colin felt there was no escape from the abuse.*

How does this affect you?

The unrelenting nature of the verbal abuse and its negative content is damaging to you. The constant barrage of abuse can cause you to change the way you view yourself. Like other forms of abuse, it encourages feelings of low self-worth. In addition, this type of abuse can change the way you view the world and, how it works, and how you fit into that world. The world seems to be a riskier and more threatening place than might otherwise be the case.

This type of abuse can cause you to feel sensitive to signs of threat. This is both because of the fact that the abuse is targeted at you and, often, your integrity, but also because it is unpredictable regarding when it will occur. This is due to the fact that it is often not related to any action on your part. It can seemingly come out of the blue.

Further, one particular difficulty is that it is not easy to know when it will end. There may be lulls in the tirade, followed by the abuser returning to the ranting abuse. In fact, victims of this type of abuse often have labelled it as more distressing than physical abuse. Typically, with physical abuse, there will be a point when the abuse starts and a definite point where that episode of abuse ends. That is, when it is over, you know that the physical abuse is finished for that time. In contrast, verbal abuse can drag on for hours or even days.

Humiliation

What is it?

This refers to a type of abuse, the purpose of which is to cause you to feel humiliated and ashamed. This might be achieved by the abuser engaging in specific actions (e.g., demanding that you wear unflattering clothing) or by the content of what is said to you (e.g., calling you demeaning names). The humiliation may be caused by experiences that take place in private, or it may be caused by the abusive partner, causing you to feel humiliated in front of others.

> *Whenever they were around friends or family, Greg's partner would make belittling comments about him. She would make comments to these people about Greg's poor sexual performance, his inability to earn enough money, his failure to be promoted, his poor social skills, and any one of numerous other complaints. The discomfort of these other people did not stop her. Greg felt humiliated. He worried about what these other people thought of him. He assumed they believed what she told them about him. Her behaviour made Greg feel small.*

How does this affect you?

Being constantly humiliated can change the way you view yourself. You come to see yourself as less worthwhile. This influences the decisions you make that affect you. These types of changes to the way you view yourself can damage your self-confidence and self-efficacy.

Further, constant humiliation that affects the way you view yourself also leaves you vulnerable to these experiences, altering how you feel. Mood changes are a common consequence of viewing yourself in a poor light.

Social isolation

What is it?

Social isolation as a form of abuse involves your abusive partner preventing you from speaking to or spending time with family and friends. This may occur directly, where you are forbidden from contacting your loved ones, or indirectly through discouraging you from having this contact or punishing you for even raising the possibility of spending time with your family or friends.

> *Brett used to have a close group of male friends. They were all good people and had been in Brett's life for many years. He was friendly with their partners, but his strongest relationships were with these men. However, from the start of his relationship with his abusive partner, she made it clear there was no place in his life for these people. She disapproved of their influence on Brett. So, increasingly, over time, she made it more and more difficult for him to spend time with his friends. She objected to any contact at all and made things difficult for Brett when they tried to contact him. Brett became so anxious about his partner's reaction to his friends that he withdrew from them. His friends gave up trying to find ways around the barriers put up by Brett's partner.*

In addition, the abusive partner might try to diminish your loved ones in your eyes. This might be achieved by telling you that your family and friends think poorly of you or by telling you that they had said negative things about your partner, causing you to support your partner over the other significant people in your life.

Alternatively, your abusive partner may have told your family and friends negative things about you in an effort to cause them to withdraw their support from you. It does not matter if what they are told is not true, their withdrawal of support causes you to be more socially isolated.

How does this affect you?

The purpose of this form of abuse is to isolate you from those who could help you or those who would offer you a frame of reference that is different from the one the abuser is presenting to you. For example, if the abuser wants you to believe they are in control and you are wrong in the way you are looking at their behaviour, they do not want others to offer you a different story than the one they are presenting.

As the abuser limits your view, you develop a smaller and more limited version of the world. It then becomes harder and harder to challenge this version. You then adopt your abusive partner's version of reality as your own. In your abusive partner's version, you are lacking in all ways, so you come to see yourself as lacking. The abusive partner comes to be seem as all-powerful.

Abduction/deprivation of liberty

What is this?

In a move to deprive you of any power in the relationship and make sure the abuser is in control you may have your ability to move freely taken away from you. This may be in the form of removing you to a different location where you know no one and from which you do not have the means to return.

You may be locked up in a room within the house or an outbuilding on your home property. Your release from these locked locations is in the control of the abuser and not up to you.

However, the deprivation of your liberty may not require that you be locked up or removed to an isolated location. The abusive partner may instil in you an understanding that you must not and cannot move beyond the limits set by the abuser without their permission.

> *Hugh and his partner lived in a remote rural area. His partner kept him under tight control. He was not allowed access to the car keys so was unable to travel anywhere without her approval. She had control of the mobile phone and, without a landline, he could not contact anyone without her permission. She would go out and leave him at home knowing that he could not go anywhere or contact anyone. She liked it this way. She made Hugh aware that she was the person who was in control.*

How does this affect you?

This type of abuse reflects a serious power imbalance in the relationship. Depriving you of your liberty makes you feel powerless and lacking in control over your own life. It gives the abuser too much power that is wielded with disregard for your well-being.

Depriving you of the freedom to come and go as you please reduces your chances of obtaining help or exposing you to different frames of reference about how other, non-abusive relationships work.

Also, depriving you of the freedom to make choices for yourself limits your life and makes it small. You live the life your abusive partner allows you but not the one you might want if circumstances were different. It is easy to come to form the view that you do not deserve the sort of life other people take for granted.

Stalking

What is it?

Here, we are referring to abusive behaviour where your partner keeps track of your every move, where you are and who you are with. This can take a number of forms, but all involve checking up on you and knowing what you are doing.

This type of abuse may take the form of your abusive partner checking your phone to see who you have contacted or who has contacted you. Any sign that you have done something that displeases your partner is used as evidence of your wrongdoing, even if the other person is the one who contacted you or nothing untoward was discussed. In the same way, your Internet and social media use can be monitored.

Your location can be monitored, either in person or with a GPS locator placed on your car or a GPS app used on your phone. In this way, wherever you are located, you can be identified at any point in time by your abusive partner.

It may also be the case that you can be physically followed. This can be done by your abusive partner or a person assigned to the task by your partner. Although it is unlikely that you would be followed all the time, the knowledge that you may be followed at any point in time creates the same sense of being under surveillance.

> *Declan had been in a relationship for over two years. During that time, his partner had kept track of his every move. At first, he wasn't aware that this was what she was doing. However, over time, there were too many coincidences, too many times when she turned up at the place he had gone, even during work hours, and too many times when she had been aware of who he had contacted and, sometimes, what he had discussed. He had caught her going through his phone, and she had hacked his email account. She had opened his mail and read his bank statements. For a long time, whenever Declan raised the issue, his partner denied keeping track of him. She would instigate an argument about a different issue, and the problem of her spying on him was never addressed. Finally, after she contacted his workplace to obtain his pay details, she admitted what she had been doing. Rather than being contrite, she was angry that Declan would challenge her right to know what he had been doing. She accused him of being untrustworthy and said she had no choice but to protect herself from his actions. Declan knew that he had done nothing wrong and was very confused by her accusations.*

How does this affect you?

When you are under surveillance and aware that your behaviour, even normal behaviour, can be used against you at any time, you are likely to feel self-conscious about everything you do. This can make you feel very anxious.

This level of monitoring can make you feel controlled and trapped. You cannot freely decide what you want to do with your day because you have to consider the consequences of what might happen should your partner be aware of your movements. This is true even when you are not doing anything that would be considered to be problematic by anyone else. It deprives you of a sense of privacy and a sense of autonomy, that is, your ability to make choices for yourself.

When you are potentially under surveillance at any time, it is very difficult for you to seek help with regard to the situation you are in. You would be running the risk of any approach to someone who can help you being found out, putting you and the person you reached out to at risk.

Economic/financial abuse

What is it?

Although it is not unusual for a couple to combine their finances, it is also usual for both partners to have a say in how their money is managed, and both parties have access to that money. As a form of abuse, the abusive partner can control all money management and distribution. Often, you would be provided with insufficient funds to run the household or engage in self-care despite the abusive partner expecting you to meet impossible standards in these areas.

Further, your abusive partner can make you answerable for every cent you spend. This may involve you having to provide receipts for every purchase or having sessions when they go through your bank statements, with you having to provide descriptions of every withdrawal.

> *Before they married, James and his partner had separate bank accounts and were in control of their own finances. Soon after they married, James' partner opened a new bank account and had James transfer his wages to that account. Soon after that occurred, James realised that the new bank account was in his wife's name only, and he could not access any funds from that account. When he raised the issue with his wife, she made it clear that she was in control of their financial state and that he no longer had any say in how the money was spent. After that, the only money he received from his wife was enough cash to purchase petrol to get to and from his place of work. She always demanded to see the receipt from those purchases to prove that he had actually spent the money on petrol. Later, when the matter came to a head, and James expressed his dissatisfaction with the arrangement, he informed his wife that he was going to have his wages paid into a separate account that he would set up. In response, his wife contacted his employer, telling him that James had a gambling problem and that they would be in dire financial difficulty if the wages did not go into the account she controlled. When James approached his boss, he denied the accusations of a gambling problem. His boss disbelieved him and kept the payment arrangement as it was. James knew he was being controlled by his wife. He had no money to do anything or go anywhere. He was too embarrassed to disclose to the people who could help him, such as his family, that he had no money. Rather than explain why he could not buy them gifts for their birthdays or at Christmas, James chose to withdraw from the family because of his embarrassment.*

How does this affect you?

Being concerned about money, even at the best of times, can make you anxious and worried. If you add the fact that you are also answerable to an abusive partner about your management of money, that anxiety must increase.

Being unable to financially support your own self-care can be humiliating as well as anxiety-provoking. Whether or not you are able to meet your own basic needs is completely in your abusive partner's control. It is a demeaning action on the part of your abusive partner to put you in a position where you have to be concerned about personal hygiene and care. The belittling nature of this form of abuse has the capacity to change how you view yourself and your sense of self-worth.

It is problematic for you to try to balance what is expected of you (e.g., provision of physical care for your abusive partner, such as preparation of meals) with your limited means to do so. It is likely to create intense feelings of anxiety when your limited financial means of providing the care is likely to trigger an abusive response in your partner.

The power imbalance in a relationship where one person has all of the control of financial matters and the other person has none is obvious. The lack of power in a relationship causes you to change how you view yourself. It can cause you to have a diminished sense of self-efficacy, which is your belief in your ability to do what you set out to do. Your inability to have control over your finances is likely to impact your belief in your capacity to care for your needs in other regards because your self-efficacy has been affected.

There are numerous other ways that abuse can manifest. The experiences of abuse form a complex pattern determined by the relationship dynamic. Each one of these types of abuse is problematic and, on the surface, seems to indicate a need to step away from the relationship. However, there are features of this complex pattern that make it difficult to walk away from the relationship.

The cycle of abuse

A good way of understanding the pattern of abuse in your relationship is to consider a four-stage cycle of abuse. By examining abuse in this way, you can begin to see how you became entangled in this type of relationship.

The four stages of the abuse cycle

There are four main stages of an episode of abuse.

Tension

Initially, there will be a build-up of tension. In an abusive relationship, it does not require that anything stressful has occurred. Rather, it is a pattern of tension increase that is determined by the psychological state of the abusive partner.

Incident

After a period of time when tension increases, which can be brief or prolonged, an abusive episode occurs. This is the climax of this build-up of tension that precedes it. It is like all the tension boils over, and there seems to be no way to avoid it or hold it back.

Reconciliation

The process of reconciliation signifies the end of the abusive episode. Although often an emotionally fraught time, it can be perceived as reassuring because you know that the abusive episode is over. The reconciliation can be characterised by apologies and reassurances that tend to make you feel better after an abusive episode, even if your experience tells you the reassurances of no further abuse are false.

Calm

After the reconciliation, you enter a period of relative calm. This is the rewarding part of the cycle, as a period of calm in an otherwise volatile relationship provides the greatest peace.

What is the impact of this cycle of abuse?

There is an important feature of this cycle of abuse that has an impact on the likelihood of you learning to tolerate abusive episodes in your relationship. If the abusive episode occurred in isolation from other events, each episode would be intolerable because they would be entirely unpredictable, and you would feel threatened all the time. However, abusive episodes do not occur separately from what precedes them or comes after them.

The feature that has the greatest influence on your ability to tolerate abusive episodes is what happens afterwards. The rewarding nature of that period of calm means that you will put up with an abusive episode because you know that a better time is coming. You know that the abuse will end and, even more importantly, it will be followed by the most rewarding time. As that period of calm following that reconciliation period is better than any other time in the relationship, it becomes desirable to have that peace and calm. As a result, you will put up with unhappy times to achieve the happiest times in your relationship.

This process can influence why you stay in a relationship that is not a healthy one for you. Let's consider the reasons why you stayed in the relationship for as long as you did.

Why did I stay?

People who have not been in an abusive relationship assume that it is a simple matter to decide to leave and end the relationship. It is likely that you have heard negative comments about people who do not leave a relationship despite being abused, made by people who have no personal experience of the matter. Even if well-intentioned, these comments typically are ill-informed and do not take into account the multitude of influences on a person in this situation. There are complex reasons people may not simply walk away.

A complicated issue

It is not unusual that after the end of an abusive relationship, you will spend some time trying to work out why you stayed as long as you did despite the ongoing abuse. The issue is complicated, and it is unlikely that there is a single reason why the relationship continued. It is also unlikely that the reasons for staying in the relationship for one person are the same as the reasons why other people stay.

Whatever the reasons, none of them will seem good enough to you to explain why you did not leave the relationship as soon as the abuse started. Nevertheless, it is worth considering some of the reasons people give for staying in an abusive relationship despite it being unhealthy.

I was too scared to leave

Often, at the beginning of a new relationship, things seem wonderful. This is true of abusive relationships. By the time you realise that you would be better off out of the relationship, it may be too late. By then, the perpetrator of the abuse may have made threats about what would happen if you ever left. You can come to believe that there would be nowhere for you to go or hide that would protect you from the perpetrator.

This fear can be the result of the work by the perpetrator to create a persona of omnipotence and omnipresence. That is, they will convince you that they have the power to cause you harm no matter what protections you have put in place and that there is no institution, such as the courts or police, that can override that power. Further, they can convince you that they have a presence, either in person or through family or associates, that will place you under surveillance no matter where you go.

It is the case that your fear about leaving may not be or may not only be about the threat to you that the perpetrator represents. You may be fearful about what would happen to other people you care about, such as your family or friends. A threat to a vulnerable family member may act as a barrier to you seeing a way to successfully separate from the perpetrator of the abuse.

Another reason you may be too scared to leave is the threats that are made in relation to the care of your children. The abuser may make threats that you will have your children taken from you and that they will remain living with the abuser. She may claim that you will not see your children again. This can feel very threatening for a person whose confidence and belief in himself have been undermined by the process of extended abuse.

> *Thomas's ex-partner had made repeated threats over the course of their relationship. She had threatened to harm their children. She had threatened to kill Thomas. She had threatened to harm his dog. She had threatened to go to the police and claim he had sexually abused their daughter. Whenever she was unhappy, she made these types of threats. She had also said that she would be the one who decided when the relationship ended, and if he tried to leave her, she would carry out these threats. Thomas felt at the time that he just couldn't take the risk of these things happening should he leave his partner.*

She said she would kill herself if I left

The fear you experienced at the thought of leaving the relationship may not only have been related to your own safety or the safety of family and friends. It also may have been related to your fear that the abuser would take their own life.

These threats of the abuser taking their own life if you do not do as they demand are reasonably common. In most instances, they represent a form of emotional blackmail and do not reflect a real intention to suicide. These threats rely on you feeling guilty at the thought of another person taking their life because of an action or failure to act on your part.

Of course, what we know about suicide threats as a form of emotional blackmail does not rule out the possibility that a person will follow through with the threat. When these suicides occur, they tend to be impulsive in nature. That is, typically, there is very little planning involved, and they are more likely to occur in the heat of the moment as emotions escalate in intensity.

This can be true, even in the context of repeated threats. As a person talks more about suicide, it becomes easier to consider ending one's own life. Then, at a time when there has been an escalation in conflict or stress, a person may then act impulsively.

Of course, none of this makes you responsible for the actions taken by another person. You cannot live your life in a way that is aimed at preventing another person from suiciding. It is not even possible to do so. If you are concerned, you would be better off asking the police to do a welfare check. They are in a much better position to obtain assistance for the suicidal individual than are you.

> *Todd learned early on in his relationship not to discuss his unhappiness or suggest that he wanted to leave. His attempts to have a conversation about the state of their relationship would result in his partner threatening to kill herself. Indeed, any comment at all about his dissatisfaction with the relationship would result in escalating threats of self-harm that were emotionally fraught, exhausting and frightening. Despite there being times when he genuinely wanted to leave the relationship, he did not want anything bad to happen to his partner. Before long, Todd learned that it was better to just keep his concerns to himself. He resigned himself to the notion that he would be trapped in the relationship forever.*

But I loved her…

Many people say they did not leave the abusive relationship because they loved their partner. Without questioning that depth of feeling, it must be considered that loving feelings in a relationship that is associated with such negative and threatening experiences are complicated ones. For those not involved, it might be hard to see how you can love someone who deliberately causes you harm.

The feelings of love can be confused by a combination of other feelings and relationship processes. When we are in a relationship with someone, we form an attachment to that person. The bond that develops is an emotional one that is built on three elements, that is, warmth (the expression of warm feelings towards each other), empathic involvement (being engaged with the person and involved in their life) and continuity of contact (regular contact and communication). This bond is difficult to break, even if your partner does terrible things. However, after the relationship is over, this attachment will end because those three elements are no longer present.

Loving feelings can be confused with feelings of dependence. Feeling like you cannot live without your partner is not the same thing as an intense feeling of love. Feelings of dependence relate to a belief that you need to rely on your partner and cannot cope without that person. However, in the case of abusive romantic relationships, these feelings can go beyond feelings of dependence and reach a feeling of anxious dependency.

Anxious dependency refers to feelings of fear at the thought of losing the relationship with the person on whom you are dependent. To stop the feelings of fear at the thought of the relationship ending, you might tolerate more abusive behaviour than you would if that fear did not exist.

Anxious dependency is often encouraged by the perpetrator of abuse. They might tell you that you cannot cope without them, that you would never cope alone, and that no other person would ever want you. These tactics are used to tie you to the abuser and to reduce the chance that you will leave.

One issue that needs to be considered is the way in which loving feelings towards an abusive partner can be misinterpreted by the person experiencing those feelings. Part of the problem with regard to misinterpreting feelings of love comes from the 'roller coaster ride' of emotions that are experienced as a result of the changing behaviours of the abuser.

If the abuser treated you badly all of the time and from the outset, you would not have stayed in the relationship. Of course, at the start of the relationship, a partner who turns out to be abusive will typically treat you well. You enter into the relationship believing that the good treatment you are receiving will continue. Then the abuse begins, sometimes building up in intensity over time or sometimes surprising you by its intensity from the first attack on you. This is often followed by a period of time when the abuser claims to be regretful and will act in a repentant way. This usually entails a period when the abuser is being nice to you.

In comparison to the dreadful experience of the abuse, those periods between the abusive episodes seem wonderful. However, typically, they are not wonderful times as would be perceived by people who are not abused. In fact, we would argue that these periods of relative calm are the absolute minimum you should expect in a loving relationship with your partner. The trouble is that you tend to misinterpret these experiences as more positive than they are by other standards, and these misinterpretations cause a strengthening of loving feelings towards your partner that, in a sense, have been falsely generated.

> *When things were bad in Kyle's relationship with his former partner, they were really bad. Her behaviour was unpredictable, volatile, and, Kyle believed, dangerous. He knew that her behaviour was having a terrible impact on him. At times, her behaviour was so out of control that he feared she would kill him. At those times, all Kyle wanted to do was escape her. However, there were times when his former partner would behave in a loving way. Indeed, there were lots of those times. Kyle would be reminded of the reasons he fell in love with her, and he would find himself feeling very protective of her, understanding that she had significant problems. He wanted to help her. He would defend her to his friends when they questioned him about her behaviour. At those times, when she was at her most loving, he could not imagine leaving his ex-partner. He loved her.*

The abuser's expressions of regret and promises of change

It is not unusual for an abusive partner to promise to change, especially immediately after an abusive episode. At these times, the abuser will seem genuinely regretful and will treat you in a loving way. They will promise that things will be different in the future. As a result, you end up feeling sorry for the abuser despite this being undeserved, and you give them another chance. Unfortunately, those promises are rarely kept.

> *When describing what had happened to him in the relationship with his ex-partner, Eric gave an account of an occasion when he was cowering in the corner while his ex-partner had repeatedly punched him. He said he had felt his eye and lip swelling. He said he remembered her shouting and foaming at the mouth because she was so angry. He remembered begging her to stop. But, the next morning, she was very remorseful, he recounted. She pleaded with him to forgive her, and she promised she would get help. She promised she would never become so out of control again. She seemed so genuine. Eric recalled a feeling of hope that sprang up inside him. He believed she intended to keep her word and do something about her problems. Despite her never seeking help, Eric still believes that her remorse was genuine and her intentions were good. After all, things did improve for a while.*

There were children involved

You may choose to stay in an abusive relationship because there are children involved. You may believe that it is not fair to the children to remove them from their mother. It is most often the case that the children will love their mother, and moving the children away from their mother seems like an unreasonable thing to do. Of course, arguments can be made about why it is an entirely reasonable course of action.

You may believe, somewhat mistakenly, that your abusive partner would never hurt the children. You may see her as a good mother. This would make it difficult for you to make a decision to take the children away from their other parent. However, good arguments can be made that the home of an abusive person is an unsafe environment for children.

Also, you may have found it difficult to leave with children for pragmatic reasons. A need to provide a stable home for children and a need to keep them fed and clothed may have encouraged you to stay in an abusive relationship for longer than you would have done had you only had your own needs to consider.

> *Rowan had children with his former partner. She had been abusive towards him throughout much of their relationship. Rowan took comfort in the fact that his partner's abuse was directed at him and not at the children. Indeed, he often described his partner as a good mother who loved and cared for the children. This was despite the fact that the children were impacted by their mother's behaviour. She often had explosive episodes when the children were present and had threatened Rowan with a knife when the children were in the room. Rowan had struggled to leave the relationship because he had not wanted to deprive the children of their mother. He knew he could not leave them in their mother's care without his protection. When he thought about leaving, he worried that, in his absence, his partner would turn her angry behaviour towards the children.*

Loss of sense of self-efficacy and self-confidence

Self-confidence refers to your belief in yourself and your view of your abilities. Self-efficacy refers to your belief in your capacity to do what you set out to do. For you to successfully navigate the demands in your life, both things need to be healthy. They allow you to believe you have the skills to deal with life problems and to follow through and resolve the problems you face.

An abusive relationship will undermine your self-confidence and self-efficacy, making it difficult for you to leave a relationship that is unhealthy for you. You struggle to believe that you would be able to look after yourself if you left the relationship.

Problems with self-efficacy and self-confidence can occur because of the messages either directly given to you by an abusive partner or from the implied messages you receive because of the abuse. Direct messages might be comments made by the abusive partner, such as telling you how stupid you are and how you cannot do anything right. Indirect messages might come in the form of an association between perceived wrongdoing (e.g., not having a meal cooked on time) and an episode of abuse where you end up criticising yourself.

What happens is that you then take on board these messages. You come to believe what your abusive partner is telling you, either through words or actions. You feel stupid. You feel that you cannot do anything without making a mistake. You certainly do not feel like you could face the demands of life alone.

> *Asher had thought often about leaving the relationship with his abusive partner. He knew what was happening to him was bad for him. He worried that he would come to serious harm. He even worried that someone would report the abuse and his partner would end up in prison. He thought that nothing good could come out of continuing the relationship. However, whenever he seriously thought about leaving, Asher was overwhelmed by all the difficulties and challenges he would face in doing so. He couldn't imagine coping with finding somewhere else to live. He was overwhelmed at the thought of having to get his possessions out of their joint property. He couldn't imagine working on a property settlement with regard to the house they jointly owned. The list of challenges seemed to be endless. Asher thought he just couldn't do any of these things. Asher considered that maybe his partner was right that he was hopeless and couldn't do anything. Maybe she had a point.*

Low sense of self-worth

Another consequence of an abusive relationship is that you can develop a low sense of self-worth. Self-worth refers to a view you have of yourself that you are good enough and worthy of being held in high regard by others. Whereas self-esteem relies on external indicators of achievement (e.g., I feel good because I got a promotion at work), self-worth is an internal view you have of yourself and your value as a person (e.g., no one would love me if they knew how useless I am).

People with low self-worth are always critically evaluating themselves, thinking they are not doing a good enough job. They focus on their mistakes, their failures and the things they did not do but maybe should have done. In relationships, people with low self-worth will go out of their way to please their partner and have a greater likelihood of tolerating neglect and abuse than do people with healthier levels of self-worth.

> *Quinn had been told often enough by his abusive partner that he was worthless. He was inclined to believe that was true. Certainly, he never seemed to be able to do anything right, as nothing he did pleased his partner... no matter how hard he tried. Quinn sometimes thought about leaving the relationship, and that gave him a moment of hope. However, he would then think that no one else would want to be in a relationship with someone as useless as him, and he couldn't bear the thought of a lifetime alone. Those hopeful thoughts of leaving were then overridden by a belief that he was better off having someone in his life than no one, even if his partner treated him badly. After all, he couldn't really expect the sort of happiness other people had because he didn't deserve it.*

Lack of social support

A perceived lack of social support can contribute to the reason why people do not feel they are able to leave an abusive relationship. Firstly, you might believe you have no one to turn to for support. This may be the result of the social isolation that was created by the limits placed on you by your abusive partner. As previously described, abusive partners tend to isolate their partners from the significant people in their lives because they do not want others to influence their partners. If that separation from the important people in your life has been occurring over a lengthy period of time, you may not feel comfortable reaching out to people whose relationship with you has diminished.

You may not have wanted to reach out to the people who used to support you, fearing that they would reject your request for help. There may be a history of your family and friends encouraging you to leave the relationship, being aware of the abuse you were experiencing. You may simply believe that these people have abandoned you because of your reluctance to take their advice. Alternatively, you may feel that your family and friends would not choose to support you because of their resentment that you have abandoned them when you were forced to withdraw at your partner's insistence.

You may have been reluctant to seek help from family and friends to leave the abusive relationship because you did not wish to disclose the abuse and involve others in the matter. You may have a genuine concern for the well-being of others, believing that by involving them, you would draw the attention of the abuser, putting them at risk. Alternatively, you simply may be embarrassed.

> *Riley was miserable. For a long time, he had put up with the abuse his partner directed towards him. Earlier on in the relationship, Riley had thought that things might improve, but he had realised, over time, that wasn't going to happen. However, the thought of actually leaving the relationship made him feel overwhelmed and lonely. Despite previously having close relationships with his family, Riley had not had any contact with them for some time. His partner had disliked him having contact with his family, and it hadn't been worth the arguments to push the point with her. Riley also felt he had no friends. His good friends had disappeared over time because his partner had hated them and reacted poorly if he had tried to see them. So, Riley felt isolated and alone. He had no one he thought would help him leave, and he wasn't sure he could do it on his own.*

As can be seen, there are complex reasons for persevering with an abusive relationship. These reasons may be ones that other people do not fully understand. There is one other aspect of abusive relationships that can have an influence on whether you have the courage to leave. This is a process engaged in by the abuser to make you feel responsible for the difficulties you experience and the failure of the relationship.

The issue of gaslighting

One important issue that needs to be discussed in relation to the impact of abuse on you and how you may need to learn to move forward is 'gaslighting'. According to the American Psychological Association, gaslighting refers to the manipulation of another person into 'doubting their own perceptions, experiences or understanding of events".

Types of gaslighting

There are four types of gaslighting. Each type has similarities with other types. Namely, they all reflect dishonesty in the effort to deny your experiences as genuine and that you are identified as the person with the problem rather than the abuser.

Outright lying

If you question a gaslighting abuser, they will lie. These lies are told with boldness and arrogance, with the goal of making you believe your concerns are unfounded and unwarranted. The lies are frequent and unrelenting. Gaslighting abusers will lie even when the lie is pointless and unnecessary.

> *Mitchell had strong suspicions that his partner was cheating on him. Then, two of his friends approached him and told him they had seen her with another man being openly affectionate. He then saw his partner with this other man. Mitchell raised the issue with his partner. She told him that there was no other man in her life, and it was not true that she had been openly affectionate with anyone. She told Mitchell he had not seen her with another man. She told Mitchell that his friends had made up the lie to hurt her. She said they were jealous of her and wanted to destroy her. She asked Mitchell if he was going to allow their jealousy and dishonesty to destroy their relationship. She asked him if he was going to let these people win. She called him a fool for believing them.*

All this lying does is create mistrust in the relationship. An abuser who gaslights should not be trusted on the basis of what they say but on their behaviour. That is, you should pay attention to what they do but not what they say.

This type of lying is a form of manipulation. It serves to isolate you from both the truth and from others who may support you. By the abuser insisting they are not at fault and the person who conveyed information to you about the abuser is wrong, you are less likely to trust your family member or friend. The abusive partner's insistence that they are telling the truth, even in the face of evidence to the contrary, encourages you to believe them. You can then feel guilty for challenging or questioning the abuser.

Manipulation of reality

This is where your experiences and perceptions are challenged by the abuser in terms of their reality. If what you think and experience is constantly challenged, you are likely to start to doubt yourself with regard to your recollections and your judgment. In the longer term, this process can have a detrimental effect on your mental health. Even if you have evidence to prove your version of events is correct, you can still come to doubt yourself and accept the gaslighting abuser's perspective. This results in you not trusting yourself to know what is accurate and inaccurate.

> *In the lead-up to his partner's birthday, Oliver asked her what she would like to do to celebrate. She told him that things would be too busy at the time of her birthday, so they might do something later in the month. He asked what she would like for a present, and she told him to buy her some perfume, and she named the type of perfume she wanted. On the day of her birthday, Oliver's partner erupted into a rage. She claimed that she had told him she wanted him to arrange to take her out for dinner for her birthday. Further, she said that she had specifically told him not to buy her perfume. Oliver didn't know how he had got it so wrong. He had been certain of what she had said, but now she was claiming that she had said the opposite. Oliver was apologetic and vowed to do better to meet her needs.*

If they believe the relationship is under threat, a gaslighting abuser may swap their approach for a period of time and agree with your version of events. They typically do this for as long as is necessary to re-establish the strength of the relationship. The effect of this switching from cold to warm behaviour can be that you begin to question whether your concerns are warranted and conclude that the state of the relationship might not be as bad as you thought.

Scapegoating

Scapegoating occurs when the gaslighting abuser holds you responsible for things they have done. The goal is to shift responsibility for wrongdoing from themselves to you in an effort to justify their behaviour. The unrelenting criticisms result in you, the scapegoat, taking on the burden of responsibility for the poor behaviour of the gaslighter. When you are put in a position of having to defend yourself for something you have not done, it is easy to be distracted from the real causes of the problem and the actual perpetrator of the wrongdoing.

> *Anthony was worried. His partner was becoming increasingly angry. She had failed to pay the car registration fee, and Anthony had been stopped by the police and fined for driving an unregistered vehicle. Anthony had reminded her the registration was due to be renewed. His partner was the person who had complete control of the finances in the home, and she always paid the bills. When his partner said she was angry with Anthony about the registration not being paid, he pointed out that she was the person who paid the bills and was in charge of the purse strings. She accused Anthony of always trying to twist things around so that it seemed like her fault when he was actually the one to blame. She kept getting angrier and louder. When he apologised and asked her not to be angry with him, she blamed Anthony for her anger. If he hadn't got them into this mess, she told him, she would not have had to become angry.*

This type of gaslighting effectively prevents good communication in a relationship. You are the person who has to constantly defend your integrity and change to improve yourself despite not being responsible for the problems that suggest the need for change. In contrast, the true perpetrator of the wrongdoing does not need to change and can adopt the stance of a long-suffering victim of your poor treatment. You feel shame, and the gaslighting abuser gets off scot-free.

Coercion

There is a range of behaviours that can be considered coercive in nature. These can range from trying to 'sweet talk' you into doing what the abuser wants, through to applying undue pressure on you in an emotionally or verbally manipulative way to do what the abuser wants, to violent and overtly bullying behaviour.

> *Brian's partner was insisting she take photographs of him engaging in sexually demeaning behaviours that he did not feel comfortable doing in any case. Not only did he feel embarrassed about having to engage in the sexual behaviours she was demanding, but he also did not trust what she intended to do with the images. He was not convinced she would not post them online or show her friends. When he begged her not to insist, his partner started by saying that he would do what she wanted if he loved her, so his refusal must mean he didn't love her. When he was still reluctant, she said he was being overly sensitive. She called him prudish and said other men would jump at the chance to do what she was asking. She then accused him of deliberately withholding love and affection and said it was unfair of him to do this, given how much she did for him. She kept up her demands until Brian agreed to do as she wished. His worry about what she was going to do with the images did not go away.*

Coercive control aims to keep the gaslighting abuser in charge, to get you to do what the abuser wants, and to make you feel dependent on the abuser for decision-making. A person who was previously self-sufficient and in charge of decisions in their life can still be vulnerable to this manipulative process.

What should I be looking for?

If you are being gaslighted, there are common things said by abusers that should ring alarm bells for you. Below are some examples with explanations of why such statements are problematic. Tick the ones you have heard said to you.

Table 1: Examples of gaslighting statements and how they affect you.

	Examples of gaslighting statements
	"What are you complaining about? I only did what I did because I was trying to help you." Statements like this challenge your view that you are justified in feeling angry about the abuser's behaviour. They aim to make you feel guilty about feeling angry. You begin to doubt the validity of your feelings. Self-doubt creeps in, and you find yourself apologising for your emotional reaction to the abuser's behaviour.
	"I don't know what you are talking about. That's not how it happened." In sometimes obvious and sometimes subtle ways, a gaslighting abuser will change the story of an event or their behaviour to suit their purposes. They will then make you believe that you are the one who is mistaken in recalling what happened. By doing this, the abuser has control over your 'reality'.
	"You are crazy." By blatantly denying your reality and identifying you as crazy for believing what you do, the gaslighting abuser wants to make you doubt yourself. Over time, this reduces your self-confidence and increases your anxiety. You start to question your interpretation of events, and the chances you will not challenge the abuser are increased.

	"Carrying on like this, it's no wonder you don't have any friends." An abuser will try to isolate you from your family and friends. They will then try to devalue you and make you feel bad about yourself for having no friends, a situation the abuser created. An abuser may even go so far as to talk to people in your life about your poor attitude, unacceptable treatment of the abuser and lack of commitment to the relationship in an effort to ensure the important people in your life are unsupportive of you. To do this, they paint themselves as the victim of your uncaring attitude and behaviour.
	"This is all your fault." Gaslighting abusers will refuse to accept blame and pass the blame onto you when it suits them to do so… which is often. Refusing to accept responsibility and blaming you for the situation creates feelings of confusion. You doubt your understanding of what is happening. When this occurs, the abuser has been successful in ridding themselves of the burden of responsibility and making you believe you have done wrong.
	"What does it matter? This isn't important." By minimising the importance of your concerns, the gaslighting abuser is trying to devalue you. They create a situation where you begin to question your own understanding of the event that has worried you. With the abuser dismissing the importance of your concern, you are likely to reach a conclusion that your reaction is excessive and unnecessary, thus distorting your sense of reality.
	"You've got it wrong. That's not what I meant." When challenged by you about a hurtful comment they made to you, a gaslighting abuser will either deny they said it or try to change the meaning of what they said. When this is done often enough, you can start to question your interpretation of what was said. This causes you to doubt yourself despite you probably being accurate in your interpretation of the intention of the comment.
	"I don't know what you are going on about. It's not that big of a deal." By diminishing the importance of your reaction to something the gaslighting abuser has said or done, the abuser is devaluing you. They try to make you feel that you have overreacted and you are the one at fault.

	"You're overreacting. You're too sensitive." In an effort to devalue you, gaslighting abusers will challenge you in terms of the intensity of your feelings, making you feel like you have been wrong to have a strong response to inappropriate behaviour on the abuser's part. Doing this increases your self-doubt and diminishes your self-worth.
	"What are you going on about? It was only a joke." Telling you that what was said was 'only a joke' is a way for a gaslighting abuser to deliver a cutting 'put-down'. By doing this, the abuser is forcing you to question your ability to distinguish between fact and fiction. It undermines your confidence in your ability to know what you are feeling is the case.
	"Stop over-analysing it." In an effort to undermine your interpretation of events relating to their behaviour, a gaslighting abuser will accuse you of holding the view you do only because you are overthinking the problem. This is a belittling action that causes you to feel less certain about your understanding of what you have experienced.
	"Nothing is going on. You are just paranoid." Rather than admit to wrongdoing, a gaslighting abuser will accuse you of being overly suspicious. In this way, they are encouraging you to believe you have made a mistake in accusing them of doing the wrong thing. You start to question the evidence on which you have based your view and, therefore, doubt yourself.
	"That didn't happen. You're just making it up." Rather than accept they have done the wrong thing, a gaslighting abuser may simply accuse you of lying when you raise an issue about their behaviour. Attempts on your part to defend yourself will cause the abuser to forcefully increase the strength of their accusation that you have fabricated the problem. This can lead to intense distress on your part that cannot be expressed easily.
	"You're just overreacting." Being told you are overreacting to something that is concerning for you in relation to your partner's behaviour is just another way of challenging the validity of your reactions.

	"I really don't know what you want me to say." When you are asking for an explanation for a partner's poor behaviour, a response of feigned confusion conveys a message that there is not anything they could say that would be acceptable to you. This transfers the responsibility for explaining the problem from the abuser to you, the person who asked for the explanation in the first place.
	"Everyone else is on my side and agrees with me." No matter how unlikely such a statement is, claiming that everyone agrees with the abuser and thus disagrees with you makes you feel everyone is against you. Gaslighting abusers make these sorts of statements to encourage you to think you are wrong and to back down and not further challenge the abuser.
	"I didn't do anything wrong. How dare you say I did." It is a more severe version of accusing you of being wrong. It makes you the target of the accusation of wrongdoing. Many people who are put in this situation end up apologising despite not engaging in the inappropriate behaviour, partly to end the accusations but also because they come to believe they might be to blame for getting the situation wrong.
	"It's not fair. I'm never allowed to let you know how I am feeling." In response to any expression by you about your concerns about their volatile behaviour, the gaslighting abuser turns the situation around and blames you for being insensitive to their needs. The goal is to move attention away from their own poor behaviour and make you feel bad.
	"Here you go again, blowing things out of proportion, just like you always do." Statements such as this cause you to question your judgment. However, making claims that you 'always' do something is bound to be an exaggeration and does not accurately reflect the situation.
	"Let's not talk about it right now." By insisting that a discussion be postponed, the gaslighting abuser is attempting to divert your focus with the hope that the issue that triggered the discussion is not discussed again. You never get the chance to express your concerns or talk about how you are feeling about a matter.

	"You don't have a clue." Telling you that you have no idea what you are talking about is a way of shutting down a discussion. A gaslighting abuser is more likely to use such a tactic if they do not like the way the conversation is going and they are struggling to find other ways of deflecting attention away from their own poor behaviour.
	"Who do you think they are going to believe, you or me?" The gaslighting abuser may ask such a question so that you doubt the degree of support you would receive for your perspective and to cause you to doubt your perspective of the abuser being the wrongdoer. However, it cannot be ruled out that the abuser actually believes that they would be perceived to be the person in the superior position, no matter how unlikely that would be the case.
	"You're going on about me, but you're not perfect, either." By pointing out your faults, the gaslighting abuser is attempting to deflect attention away from the actual topic of discussion, that is their behaviour. You then are put into a position where you either have to defend yourself or accept that you have no right to raise a complaint about your partner's behaviour.
	"Let's just forgive and forget and move on." The goal of the gaslighting abuser is to shut down the discussion. However, it also puts the burden of responsibility on you to be the one who lets go of an issue that concerns you without the abuser having to do anything.
	"Not this again. You are always going over the past." No gaslighting abuser wants to revisit the past. In fact, they would rather rewrite the past to cast themselves as the hero and reinterpret their role in events that you recall as abusive. If done in the way the abuser wants, you will come away feeling like you are the one causing the problem.
	"After all that I've done for you, is this how you treat me?" The goal here is to divert attention from the poor behaviour of the gaslighting abuser and onto you. In doing this, the abuser is trying to create a situation where you feel guilty and are likely to back off from any challenge in relation to the abuser's behaviour.
	"We have been over this already. I can't believe you don't remember." Here, the gaslighting abuser is trying to rewrite history and pretend that the matter has been resolved. It is a strategy used by the abuser to make you question your memory.

	"Here we go again. You always have to be right." Despite the fact that it is the gaslighting abuser who always has to be right, they try to make out this is a shortcoming you possess. In doing so, they are encouraging you to form the view that you are the one being unreasonable.
	"There is something wrong with you. You need to get some help." In an effort to invalidate what you are thinking and feeling and to move the attention away from their actions and onto your mental health, the gaslighting abuser will try to make you feel like 'normal' people would not think the way you do.
	"What an imagination!" This statement has the same effect as telling you that you are making things up. It is a deflection technique used by the gaslighting abuser to make you question your interpretation of events.
	"You always think you're so smart." Such a statement is designed to convey the opposite, that you are not smart and you are mistaken about the views you are holding. This tactic is aimed at devaluing you and causing you to back down from questioning the actions of the abuser.
	"I don't know what you are talking about. You're not making sense." The purpose here is to make you feel uncertain about your ability to convey your concerns. However, the underlying goal is to take the focus away from your concerns and place it on your capacity to communicate what you are trying to say.
	"What are you doing? You are just trying to confuse me." Gaslighting actions and comments are designed to confuse you and distract you from what the gaslighting abuser is trying to do. A claim that you are trying to confuse them typically has no basis.
	"Get your facts straight." This is another way of getting you to question yourself. By simply denying that what you are saying is the truth, the gaslighting abuser is attempting to deflect attention away from their own problematic behaviour.

	"You never said that." / "I never said that." The goal here is to get you to doubt your memory of events. Such tactics try to make you feel like you do not have a grip on your recall or your sanity.

Checklist version available at elemen.com.au

As you can see, there are many ways in which an abusive partner can gaslight you. All are dishonest representations of what actually happened, and they are all designed to throw you off balance.

Indicators of gaslighting and the effects on you

Before moving on, let's consider whether you have been on the receiving end of gaslighting by your abusive partner and whether it has affected your mental health.

	Indicators of gaslighting and the effects on you
	Have you been having trouble making decisions, even simple ones?
	Have you often made excuses to your family and friends about your partner's behaviour?
	Are you constantly having to second-guess yourself?
	Have you blamed yourself for your partner treating you badly?
	Have you tried to convince yourself that your partner's poor behaviour is not really that bad?
	Have you had to walk on eggshells around your partner?
	Have you questioned yourself about whether you are too sensitive?
	Have things your partner said caused you to question the validity of your thoughts, feelings, judgments, and observations?
	Did you feel lonely and trapped in your relationship with your partner?
	Have you doubted your own memory and your sanity?

	Have you ever just kept quiet with your partner when you felt you should have spoken up about what you believed or thought?
	Have you felt on edge much of the time and threatened?
	Have you felt that your partner might be correct when she accused you of being stupid or crazy?
	Have you thought that you just cannot do anything right and felt disappointed in who you turned out to be?
	Did you spend a lot of time apologising for your actions even though it was not really necessary to apologise?

Checklist available at elemen.com.au

Gaslighting can have a profound and ongoing effect on how you view yourself and how you trust your own feelings, thoughts and memories. These effects then need to be undone. We will consider ways to challenge the effects later in this workbook.

My reaction to the end of the relationship

Here, we need to briefly consider your reaction to the end of the relationship. Dealing with the aftermath can be as difficult as dealing with the relationship while you are in it.

The abuser ended the relationship

When it is the abuser who ended the relationship, you are faced with the challenge of dealing with the fact that you have lost something that you once thought you could not cope without. Often, you are ill-prepared to deal with the abrupt end of the relationship. You have had no time to consider this happening, and you are not in your best frame of mind to cope with the challenges associated with a relationship ending. When you are at your lowest ebb, you then have to deal with additional problems.

Of course, the fact that your abusive partner ended the relationship does not mean that she will move on and leave you to recover. She can still continue to expect to have control over you and what you do. She can still seek to torment you because she believes it is her right to do so. This can create additional problems for you at a time when you are trying to get your life back on track.

You ended the relationship

Even if it is the case that you ended the relationship, you can still face a period of difficult adjustment. You need to work on undoing the psychological damage done to you. The challenge of moving forward can be made more difficult because you have to work on reaching a point where you feel able to take charge of your life again.

You also have additional worries about the threats that may have been made to you in anticipation of you ending the relationship. You have a need to protect yourself in case your abusive former partner follows through with those threats. Just as may occur when the abuser ends the relationship, your former partner may not leave you alone to get on with your life. Her inability to accept your decision may cause her to act in ways that make your adjustment more challenging.

Grief and disenfranchised grief

Although your relationship with your abusive ex-partner was a difficult one, it is worth taking a moment to consider that you may react to the loss of that relationship with feelings of grief.

What is grief?

Grief is a universally experienced emotional reaction in response to loss or perceived loss. It can also be experienced in relation to expected loss (anticipatory grief) or in situations where you or others might not recognise that grief is warranted (disenfranchised grief). Grief is experienced in relation to the loss of someone or something important to you. For example, you may grieve the loss of a future you expected to have available to you but did not turn out the way you wanted.

Typically, grief is experienced in stages. Acute grief occurs in that initial period after the experience of loss. These feelings of grief occur irrespective of the event that triggered it. This type of grief is associated with severe or intense feelings of distress.

In the initial phase of acute grief, you can feel shock and numbness. You feel disengaged from what is happening. This dissociative experience is protective, in a sense, shielding you from the intensity of the emotional reactions to the loss. However, there will come a time when the full strength of your emotional reactions will be felt.

The emotional reactions to the loss you have experienced can be varied and may change over the course of the period of acute grief. Although we typically associated grief with feelings of sadness, grief can also be related to feelings of anger, guilt, anguish, regret or relief, depending on the circumstances of the loss and all the things that came before.

These emotional reactions to loss can be painful. At the beginning, they may seem to be always present. However, before long, this changes and you experience the feelings of grief in bursts or waves. These waves of grief tend to be triggered by specific reminders of your loss or things that make you think about the person in the context of better times.

These waves of grief do lessen over time, both in terms of their frequency of occurrence and in their strength or intensity. This reduction will allow you to regain a feeling of emotional balance. At this time, your attention will be more focused on events outside of you rather than being focused on your emotional state.

The next phase is what is known as integrated grief. This is experienced after you transition beyond the acute grief stage. To reach a point of integrated grief, it may take you several months or more or may occur sooner.

There are signs that you have moved to integrated grief. For example, you will be able to think about the person or what you have lost without the overwhelming nature of your earlier emotional responses. You can pick up your life again, returning to work and engaging in activities that give you pleasure.

It is often the case that you can move forward with a better perspective on life, a greater understanding of what is important in life, and a new focus on the things that matter. These positive changes in outlook have been identified to occur after a serious and often traumatic life event or events. These life events act as a catalyst for you to change your outlook on life. It causes you to reprioritise things so that your focus is more on the important issues in your life and less on the more minor things that no longer seem to matter.

For most people, this is the point where you move on with your life, being the new person you have become as a result of the loss you have experienced. However, for a small number of people this is more challenging to achieve. For those people, complicated grief is experienced when people struggle to overcome their acute grief phase. The feelings of longing and loss do not abate over time. However, complicated grief is not the typical outcome of a grieving process. Most people transition through to a point where they can experience life in a meaningful way.

Disenfranchised grief

One of the factors that can make grieving more difficult is when the grief you experience is disenfranchised. What does this mean? Disenfranchised grief is when your grief reaction does not fit with society's expectations. Our society has created certain expectations regarding how people grieve and about what they should grieve. When the trigger for your grief or the way in which you are grieving does not fit with those societal expectations, you can feel disenfranchised.

Disenfranchised grief can occur in numerous contexts. Importantly for our discussion here, your grief over a loss that is not death (e.g., the loss of a relationship), your grief for something that did not actually occur (e.g., loss of a future you hoped to have), or grief for the loss of a loved one from your life even though that person abused you and caused you harm are all likely to disenfranchise your grief. In all of these cases, it is hard to obtain the same sort of sympathy and support that are received by people who are grieving a loss in more societally approved ways or because of experiences society sees as acceptable reasons for grieving.

Certainly, even though this is not true, disenfranchised grief is typically considered to be less important or less significant than more commonly accepted grief. As a result, you can experience disregard for your feelings. As a consequence of this disregard, you can be denied the right to mourn in the usual sense or in the way you would normally choose to mourn.

Of course, disenfranchised grief does not make the grief less real for you. The fact that others do not validate your feelings does not mean they are not legitimate. It may mean that you will need to seek other avenues for expressing your grief or other ways of seeking the help and support you need. Consider the following ways of helping you cope.

Table 2: Ways of coping with disenfranchised grief.

Seek out supportive people who understand what you are experiencing.   These might be people who have experienced a similar grief experience or they may be people who understand what you have lost and how important this loss is to you. They may also be people who have a more thorough understanding of your relationship so appreciate the value to you of aspects of the relationship you have lost.
Create a mourning ritual that is important to you.   Rituals are often important in the mourning process. In the absence of other means of expressing your grief, you may keep items that have a sentimental value. You may prepare an album of photographs of important events in your relationship. You might write a farewell letter to your ex-partner without any intention of ever sending it.
Ask for the help you need.   Without having to disclose the reasons why you are seeking assistance, you can still ask for help. Let your support network of family and friends know when you need company, when you need to be distracted by an activity, or when you need someone to listen to you talk.
Seek professional help.   When you need to discuss your grief in a non-judgmental environment, professional help can provide you with that opportunity. Seeking professional help can also assist you in normalising your grief so that you see it is a natural reaction to loss despite the rejection of this by others.

So, you have experienced the abuse and your emotional reaction to it. The effects on you can feel quite profound. What do you do about it now?

What do I need to do now?

So, what do you do now that the relationship has ended? Let's consider what you may need.

> We will be making some comments about how to protect yourself and keep yourself safe. We will direct you to information about things you can do for yourself as well as services you may choose to access.
>
> We will teach you to manage the anxiety you feel. We will provide you with information about how your nervous system functions and give you reasons why your nervous system is in an overly aroused state. This will be followed by introducing you to ways you can control what your nervous system is doing as well as inviting you to learn to quiet your mind so that you can control your distress.
>
> Following from this, we will apply some of these skills to the management of sleep disturbance if you are having trouble with insomnia. We will explain your sleep cycle and provide you with reasons why your sleep is disturbed. We will then introduce some simple strategies for helping you sleep better.
>
> We will then introduce you to the notion of coping and explore your preferred ways of coping with life problems. We will then show you ways to build on your effective coping strategies or build new and better ones.
>
> Attention will then be given to the way you think and how errors in thinking can affect how you feel and behave. These errors in thinking can have their foundation in the types of experiences you have had in the abusive relationship and the messages you received from your abusive partner, how you view your place in the world, and how you view your future. After an abusive relationship, you can view the world as more threatening, yourself as less worthy, and the future as more dangerous and unpredictable than necessary.
>
> When you have learned ways to improve your thinking, you can pay some attention to re-establishing your sense of self and your self-worth. These are particular aspects of you that are often affected by abusive experiences. Indeed, the actions of your abusive partner could have deliberately targeted these areas in an effort to undermine you.
>
> We then will focus on rebuilding your self-efficacy. This is your belief that you can achieve what you set out to do. Self-efficacy is often damaged by the messages you have received in your relationship that you are incapable and incompetent.
>
> After being treated in an invalidating, denigrating and demeaning way, it can be difficult to understand your rights. We will cover your basic rights that you are entitled to defend.
>
> Then, we will teach you ways to assertively stand up for your rights. We will cover ways you can ask for change and negotiate for a good outcome. This is important

after a period of time when your wishes were dismissed or considered secondary to your abusive partner's wishes.

Finally, we will consider ways you can improve the quality of life. This can help you regain the things in your life that you value the most.

Keep yourself safe

Here, we would like to emphasise the importance of keeping yourself safe. Because the steps you should take are not strictly a psychological issue, rather than cover all the things you need to do, we would like to direct you to a website, yourtoolkit.com, that provides a comprehensive account of what you need to do and the resources available to you in Australia should you need to access them. The information about what you need to do is relevant for people wherever you live. However, if you live in a country other than Australia, look for other similar websites that can provide you with information about specific services that are available to you.

yourtoolkit.com

Consistent with the information contained on this website and to give you an idea of the things you need to consider, we have provided a checklist of the information you might need to ensure your personal safety and to look after yourself in the aftermath of the end of an abusive relationship. We refer you to the website mentioned above to examine the information and tips in relation to each of these areas.

Self-protection checklist	
In the early stages	
	Learn ways to stay safe online, including by using hardware (phones, computers, devices) and online accounts (email, social media, location safety).
	Make a safety plan for yourself, your children and your pets.
	Keep important documents safe or copies of important documents (financial, legal, business).
	Collect any evidence you might need for Family Court applications.
	Prepare your banking details (opening new accounts, freezing and closing joint accounts).

Things to do immediately	
	Explore government assistance and benefits available to you.
	Explore family violence restraining orders.
	Investigate and take advantage of assistance services available in your community.
Rebuilding your life	
	Make sure you are safe at home (safety improvements you can make or Safe at Home programmes you can access).
	Make sure you are safe in public (in public places, at work, when driving).
	Make sure your mail is safe.
	Seek financial support available for people who have experienced family and intimate partner violence.
	Secure safe housing/tenancy.
	Access legal services if needed.
Moving forward	
	Learn to budget.
	Adopt strategies to save some money.
	Explore credit alternatives.
	Learn to manage your debt.
	Understand your tax obligations and tax relief.
	Establish a superannuation/retirement account.

	Explore insurance options.
	Prepare a will.
	Effectively use financial settlements.

Checklist available at elemen.com.au

Manage your anxiety/trauma

Now, we can move on to the psychological aspects of you learning to cope in the aftermath of the breakdown of your abusive relationship. We are going to start by teaching you about your nervous system and how to control it. This is important because most people who have experienced abuse in a relationship have also experienced an impact on their nervous system arousal. So, let's have a look at how your nervous system works and how it reacts to stressful events.

What is your nervous system doing?

Your autonomic nervous system (ANS) is the part of your nervous system that drives your functioning. It regulates how your body works and makes adjustments that are required for you to function on a moment-by-moment basis.

Your ANS is divided into two parts: the parasympathetic nervous system and the sympathetic nervous system. Your parasympathetic nervous system is the part of your ANS that should be driving you most of the time. It makes sure everything is ticking along so that your body gets what it needs and you can function well.

Your sympathetic nervous system has a specialised function. It is your self-protection system that automatically activates when you are under threat. So, if you were crossing the road and a truck came screaming around the corner, your sympathetic nervous system would activate so that you could quickly and efficiently move out of the way of the truck and reach safety. Adrenaline would release into your system, causing your hands to shake and your heart rate to increase, but you would reach the safety of the footpath on the other side of the road, and you would be fine. Your brain would then recognise that you are safe, your sympathetic nervous system would turn off, and your parasympathetic nervous system would take over again.

Your sympathetic nervous system is attuned to your brain perceiving signs of threat. It activates when you are at risk of harm and prepares you to deal with that threat. It is an effective self-protection system when you are under threat. Unfortunately, for people who develop an overly sensitive sympathetic nervous system as a result of repeated exposure to danger and threat, or at times when they are experiencing significant stress in their lives, their sympathetic nervous system will activate at the slightest indication that something is wrong and will prepare them to deal with the threat. This can occur even when there really is no threat to manage. This is what happens when you are anxious in the absence of an obvious cause of your anxiety or an obvious sign of immediate danger. In effect, your brain cannot distinguish between an external threat (e.g., a truck coming around the corner) and an internal threat (e.g., you thinking worrying or anxiety-provoking thoughts). An overly sensitive nervous system will rely on its self-defence mechanism to protect you from perceived harm.

Your nervous system will also react to events that are crises in your life that do not present the same level of threat as physical abuse, for example. Although the experience of emotional abuse is stressful, this type of abuse itself is not physically threatening to you. Nevertheless, your sympathetic nervous system can be triggered by emotional abuse. As stated, your brain cannot always make a distinction between an external threat to your physical integrity and a threat to your emotional well-being that is internally generated.

Below is a table providing an overview of the activities of the parasympathetic and sympathetic nervous systems.

Table 3: The functions of the parasympathetic and sympathetic nervous systems.

	Parasympathetic	Sympathetic
Eyes	Constricts pupils	Dilates pupils
Salivary glands	Stimulates salivation	Inhibits salivation
Heart	Slows heartbeat	Accelerates heartbeat
Lungs	Constricts bronchi	Dilates bronchi
Stomach	Stimulates digestion	Inhibits digestion
Liver	Stimulates bile release	Simulates glucose release
Kidneys		Stimulates release of adrenaline and noradrenaline*
Intestines	Stimulates peristalsis and secretion	Inhibits peristalsis and secretion
Bladder	Contracts bladder	Relaxes bladder

* Also known as epinephrine and norepinephrine

So, when your sympathetic nervous system is activated, a series of physical changes occur that make sense if they are in response to a threat to your physical integrity.

> Adrenaline is released so that you are alert and in a heightened state, ready to deal with the threat. This causes your heart rate to increase and can cause your hands, or even your whole body, to shake.

> Your hearing and your eyesight become better than normal. Everything sounds louder than it really is, and it is difficult to tolerate lots of light and movement. This is why anxious people tend to avoid places like supermarkets. Too much noise, too much

light, and too much movement can be overwhelming when you feel anxious. Anxious people tend to tolerate these things poorly because of the acuteness of their senses when their sympathetic nervous systems are activated.

In our view, the most amazing thing that happens is that your sympathetic nervous system shuts down the systems it does not need to be using. For example, when under threat, your body needs to produce lots of glucose for energy, so it stimulates glucose production. However, other systems that are not needed are shut down. In particular, your sympathetic nervous system shuts down your gastrointestinal system (e.g., inhibits digestion and inhibits peristalsis and secretion, with peristalsis referring to the contraction of the muscles that push forward the contents of your digestive tract). This is all right if it is shut down for the period of time it takes for you to deal with a truck coming around the corner. Your body copes less well with your gastrointestinal system not functioning if the sympathetic nervous system activation is prolonged. You can lose your appetite, experience nausea, develop diarrhoea or constipation, and you can experience difficulty eating, or you will overeat to try to control the uncomfortable state of your digestive system.

All of these symptoms make sense if you are under threat but become a problem if the activation of your sympathetic nervous system is prolonged. Also, when your sympathetic nervous system is activated for reasons other than obvious threat, you can develop a sense of imminent danger just because your sympathetic nervous system has taken over your functioning. When your sympathetic nervous system is activated, your brain will interpret this as a sign that something is wrong. You will develop an overwhelming feeling that something terrible is about to happen, even in the absence of an identifiable sign of threat.

Later, we will introduce some straightforward ways you can bring your sympathetic nervous system under better control so your anxiety and fear are reduced. You can learn to control the messages being received because you are worried so that the message is not misinterpreted, and you can avoid the sense that something terrible is going to happen.

Range of arousal

As described earlier, it is likely that your sympathetic nervous system has been responding to your current situation as if it was an immediate threat to your physical integrity. When this occurs, you experience a number of physical changes that place your system into a self-protective state. You need strategies that will send a message to your nervous system that you are safe.

Before considering ways to achieve this, we need to look at one other feature of your nervous system. It is worth noting that human beings have a range of nervous system arousal within which we function the best. This range is quite large, from low in the range when we are very relaxed to high in the range when our nervous system is most 'revved up' but still manageable. Pictured below is a diagram of this arousal range. The range within which you function best is known as the *window of tolerance*.

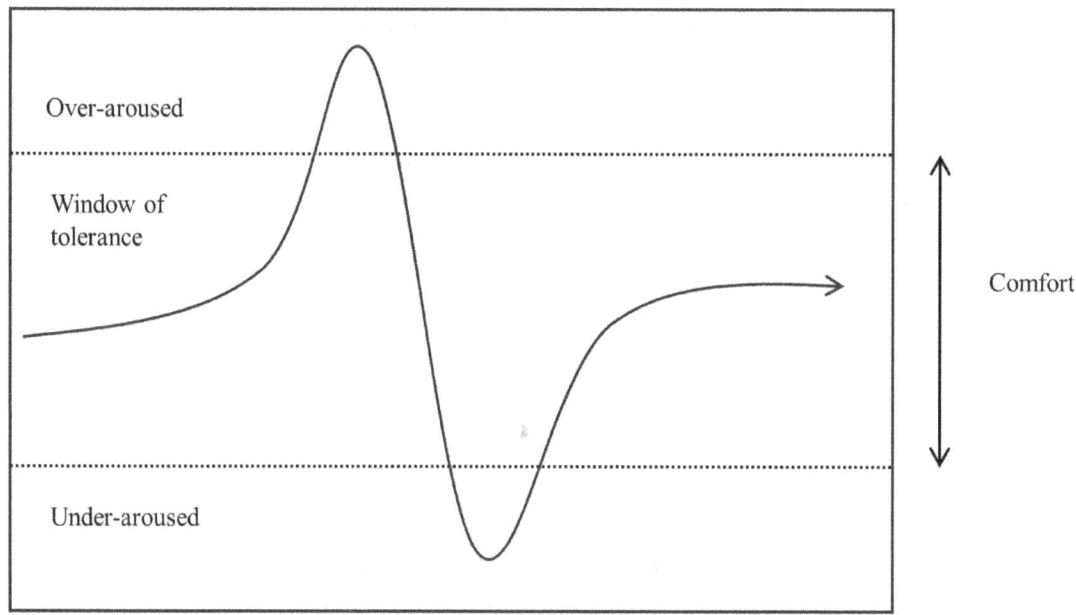

Figure 1: A diagram of the window of tolerance.

Within this window of tolerance, you have the flexibility to respond to the demands being placed on you. In this way, your arousal level will increase when you are faced with a demand and then decrease when that demand is over. As long as your arousal stays within this window, you will respond well to pressures placed on you.

If your arousal level drops below the lowest point of that range, you will enter a state of hypoarousal. In this state, you will feel slowed down and lethargic. Your functioning at this point will be inadequate, and your ability to respond to demands will be poor. If your arousal increases beyond the ceiling level, you will enter a state of hyperarousal. When this occurs, you can feel too aroused and can feel anxious and panicky. Your functioning will be impacted, and your ability to cope with pressures will deteriorate.

When you have been too stressed for a while or when you are faced with significant challenges but are still managing to cope, your arousal level creeps up from an optimal level of arousal in the middle of the window of tolerance to the upper extremes. You will find that you cannot or do not reduce that high level of arousal, even when you should be able to let go. This is why people cannot sleep well when they are under pressure. They can never relax enough for their arousal to decrease to a comfortable state. So, your 'baseline' arousal level, which is the starting point from which you respond to life demands, is high up in the range instead of midway.

In this case, your arousal level remains elevated. You barely notice this because it starts to feel normal to be under that much stress with your arousal level that high. But a problem exists. When any other thing occurs to which you have to respond, your arousal level will increase to deal with that additional demand being placed on you. However, when the starting point of your arousal level, or your baseline arousal level, is already so high, you have no room to move. Any increase in arousal will push you through the ceiling and into an uncomfortable and unpleasant hyperaroused state. You will experience anxiety as a result.

Your high starting point gives you no flexibility to respond or react to even minor additional stressors. So, the ways you normally cope with demanding situations fail because you have moved out of the range where you can successfully apply your usual coping strategies.

Anxiety management strategies

Your goal should be to get your nervous system back under control. Dealing with the challenges you have faced in relation to the abuse you experienced has likely pushed your arousal level to the upper limits of your window of tolerance. Extra demands, even minor ones, then cause your arousal level to move beyond the ceiling of the window of tolerance and uncomfortable and unpleasant anxiety symptoms are then experienced.

You need to aim to bring your optimal arousal level down to at least the middle of the window of tolerance, with a baseline or starting point, when you are at your most relaxed, to the lower end of that range. You need to teach your nervous system to have a better starting point and a better optimal arousal level.

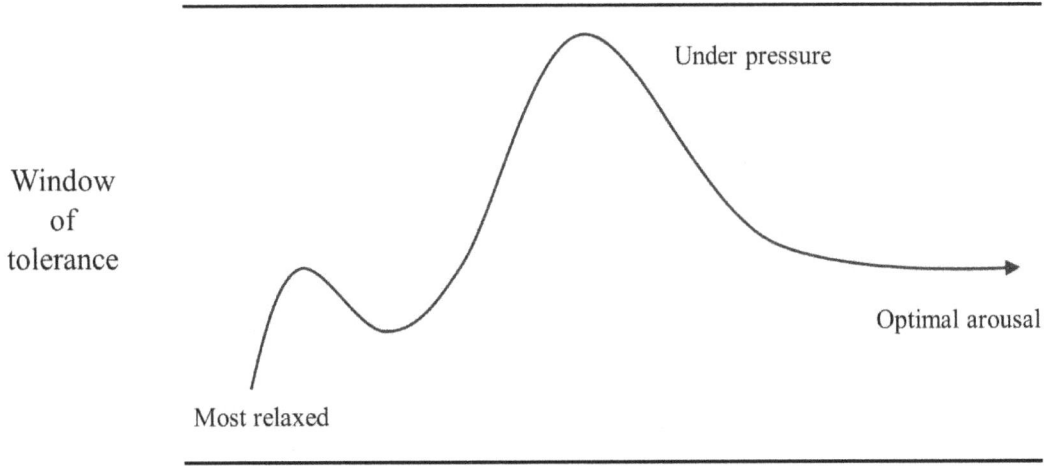

Figure 2: A diagram of an optimal level of arousal.

How do you achieve this? Consider the following. When you are in an elevated or heightened state, at the top of your window of tolerance or beyond it, your heart rate increases and your breathing changes. Your heart rate elevation is caused by a release of adrenaline that occurs when your sympathetic nervous system is triggered. This can be very uncomfortable, and it feels like there is very little you can do about it. However, there are things you can do to bring this under control.

Your breathing changes contribute to the elevation in your heart rate. When people are stressed, their breathing tends to be rapid and shallow. You can liken this pattern of breathing to the waves on top of the water. Form a picture in your mind of the way a child draws waves. When you are stressed, you tend to breathe in sharply, then breathe out quickly and then breathe in again quickly. You tend not to breathe all the way out before you breathe in again. This inhalation-exhalation pattern is what affects your heart rate.

In contrast, when you are relaxed, your breathing tends to be deeper and slower and has a pattern than is similar to the swell in the ocean. The inhalation-exhalation pattern is a comfortable breath-in followed by a long, slower breath-out. You do not breathe in again until you have breathed all the way out.

From the diagram below, you can see the pattern of anxious, rapid and shallow breathing on the top. Below that is the pattern of slower, deeper breathing that is characteristic of a more relaxed state.

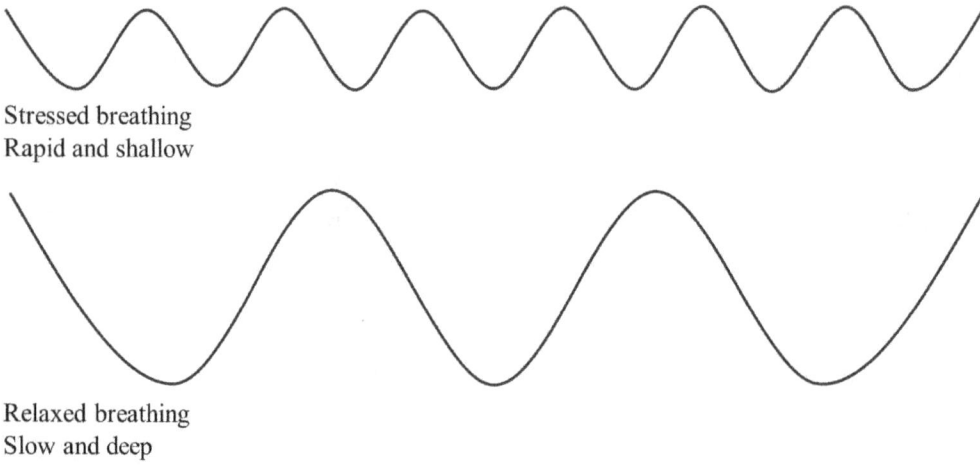

Figure 3: A comparison between stressed and relaxed breathing.

The reason your breathing pattern affects your heart rate is because these two things are linked. Under normal, stress-free conditions, you heart rate increases as you breathe in and then slows as you breathe out. This is normal. When you are stressed and your respiration rate increases and your breathing is shallower, your heart rate does not have a chance to slow before you breathe in again. Therefore, your heart rate is elevated and stays elevated.

Let's, for a moment, go back to the truck speeding around the corner, threatening to run you over. Your sympathetic nervous system is activated, allowing you to be in the right physical state to move quickly out of harm's way and protect yourself. When you get to the other side of the road, the truck goes past, and you are unharmed; your brain registers these experiences, and your sympathetic nervous system turns off, and your parasympathetic nervous system takes over. This is because reaching the other side of the road and seeing the truck pass you by are safety signals. Your brain interprets these signs as indicators that you are going to be all right as danger has passed.

Of course, no such safety signals are available when you are sitting in your loungeroom worrying or shopping at the supermarket. They are not that sort of event. Also, there are no safety signals when your nervous system has learned to be on alert because of abuse in a relationship. Your brain would struggle to identify safety indicators because they do not exist in that sort of form. Even after the abusive relationship is over, your nervous system is slow to get the message you are safe. It has been on red alert for so long that it does not know how to let go. What you can do when this occurs is to offer your brain a safety signal of a different type.

You can send a message that everything is all right by deliberately slowing your heart rate from its elevated rate to a more normal rate for you. Although it sounds difficult to achieve, that is controlling your heart rate, it actually is a reasonably straightforward undertaking. If you slow your breathing and lengthen your exhalation until you have breathed all the way out before breathing back in, your heart rate will come into line with your breathing rate, and your heart rate will go down.

To use our waves and ocean swell analogy, the aim is to change the pattern of your breathing from waves on the top of the water to a pattern like the swell in the ocean, where the water is lifted up and then put back down as the swell passes. You are aiming for an easy, comfortable breath in, followed by a long, slow breath out.

The ideal situation is to breathe out for twice as long as it takes you to breathe in. Elongating your exhalation requires that you slow the amount of air you breathe out so that you can breathe out for longer. You should aim to breathe all the way out, emptying your lungs, before you gently and comfortably breathe back in.

This pattern of breathing should result in a slowed heart rate and a subsequent reduction in that sense of anxiety or crisis that occurs when your sympathetic nervous system is triggered. This occurs because your brain interprets the reduction in heart rate and the change in breathing pattern as a signal that the crisis is over.

Let's consider a simple exercise to control your breathing by deepening your breaths and slowing them down.

	Slowing and controlling your breathing
1.	Without trying to change your breathing, just notice for a moment the pattern of your inhalations and exhalations.
2.	Now, take a comfortable breath in. It does not have to be too deep, but rather just a comfortable breath.
3.	Now, breathe out, slowing the amount of air you exhale and lengthening your breath as a result.
4.	When your lungs feel empty of air, gently and comfortably breathe back in.
5.	As you breathe, practice lengthening your exhalation just a bit. You may also deepen your breath in slightly. Keep in mind the picture of the ocean swell if this helps.
6.	Practice this pattern of breathing for as long as you feel comfortable.

Exercise available at elemen.com.au

There is another element that you can add to this breathing exercise that may help with your ultimate goal of reducing your anxiety and signalling your sympathetic nervous system to turn off so your parasympathetic nervous system can do its job. You can include in this breathing exercise the element of reducing your muscle tension.

People who are stressed tend to have tense muscles. Although this muscle tension can occur anywhere in the body, common sites include the forehead and scalp, neck, jaw, shoulders, and chest. The increased muscle tension contributes to the overall sense of readiness to deal with threat. On the downside, tense muscles can cause headaches, chest and other pain.

If tense muscles present a significant problem for you, then a progressive muscle relaxation exercise may help. A general overview of this technique is provided below, along with a more comprehensive version. However, another easy strategy is to link the relaxation of muscles with the breathing exercise.

As you breathe out, just relax your muscles in places where they feel tight and tense. You do not have to achieve marked muscle relaxation to experience a noticeable difference. Just drop your shoulders, relax your jaw, smooth your forehead or relax your stomach muscles. Aim for a gentle relaxation of tight muscles as you exhale.

The combination of breathing exercises and muscle relaxation can be used even when the focus is on controlling your breathing. You can also use the combined technique when your primary focus is on troubling muscle tension. In combination, the techniques can help with either target.

	Combined breathing and muscle relaxation technique
1.	Take a comfortable breath in. It does not have to be too deep, rather just a comfortable breath.
2.	Now, breathe out, slowing the amount of air you exhale and lengthening your breath as a result. As you breathe out, drop your shoulders, relax your jaw, smooth your forehead and relax your abdominal muscles.
3.	When your lungs feel empty of air, gently and comfortably breathe back in.
4.	As you breathe, practice lengthening your exhalation just a bit. You may also deepen your breath in slightly. Keep in mind the picture of the ocean swell if this helps. Continue to relax your muscles slightly on each exhalation.
5.	Practice this pattern of breathing and muscle relaxation for as long as you feel comfortable.

Exercise available at elemen.com.au

As stated, if muscle tension presents you with a significant problem, you may wish to try a method of progressive muscle relaxation. People with muscle tension problems often feel pain from strained muscles, tension headaches, pain in the neck and shoulders and/or sore muscles across the chest. Tensing your muscles before relaxing them has a number of purposes. It helps you to clearly identify where the tension in your body is located. It helps you feel the difference between a tense muscle and a relaxed one, which is helpful when the muscle has been tense for a long time. Finally, tensing the muscle first helps to induce deeper relaxation in that muscle when you relax it. To address the problem of tense muscles, we will start with a longer version that will help you learn the technique. You can then change to a shorter version, which we describe below.

	Progressive muscle relaxation (longer version)
1.	Choose a comfortable place where it is quiet. Lay down or sit in a comfortable position with your feet flat on the floor.
2.	Now, clench both your fists… tighter and tighter. Notice the tension in your muscles. Keep them clenched for about 10 seconds. Now relax. Feel your muscles relax. Notice the difference between the tension and relaxation.
3.	Repeat the procedure with your fists. Notice the difference between tension and relaxation.

4.	Now, bend your elbows on both arms and tense your biceps. Hold the tension. Now relax. Notice the difference between tension and relaxation.
5.	Repeat the procedure with your elbows bent and your biceps tensed. Hold the tension, then relax. Pay attention to the change from tension to relaxation.
6.	Now, frown as hard as you can. Notice the tension in your forehead. Hold the tension. Now relax. Notice the difference you feel after you have released the tension.
7.	Now, frown again as hard as you can. Hold the tension, then release it. Notice the contrast between tension and relaxation.
8.	Now, close your eyes and squint them tightly. Hold the tension, then relax. Allow your eyes to achieve a comfortable, relaxed state. Notice the change. Repeat by closing your eyes and squinting, then relaxing and letting go of the tension.
9.	Now, clench your jaw. Bite down. Notice the tension throughout your jaw. Now, relax your jaw, allowing your teeth to fall apart slightly. Notice the feeling of relaxation. Repeat this exercise with your jaw.
10.	Now, press your tongue hard against the roof of your mouth. Hold it there. Feel the tension at the back of your mouth. Now relax. Notice the difference between the tension and relaxation. Repeat the exercise with your tongue.
11.	Now, purse your lips, pushing them out into an 'O' shape. Hold them there. Now release the tension and relax. Notice how your mouth feels now that it is relaxed. Repeat the exercise with your lips.
12.	Now press your head back as far as it will comfortably go. Hold onto the tension. Roll your head from the right to the left, allowing the focus of the tension to change. Now relax. Feel the difference between the tension in your neck and the relaxation. Repeat the exercise by pressing your head back.
13.	Now, bring your head forward with your chin on your chest. Feel the tension in your throat and the back of your neck. Hold the tension, then relax and allow your head to return to a comfortable position. Repeat the exercise by bringing your head forward.

14.	Now, shrug your shoulders, bringing your shoulders up and allowing your head to hunch down between them. Hold the tension. Now relax and notice the difference between tension and relaxation.
15.	Now, breathe in deeply and hold your breathe. Hold it. Now allow yourself to gently exhale, letting go of tension as you breathe out. Feel your body relax. Repeat the exercise, breathing in then gently letting go.
16.	Now, tense your stomach muscles. Hold onto the tension. Now relax. Let your stomach muscles relax and appreciate that feeling. Repeat the exercise with your stomach muscles.
17.	Now, arch your back without straining. Hold onto the tension. Now, let it go. Notice the change in your muscles. Now repeat the exercise by arching your back.
18.	Now, tighten your buttocks and thighs. Press down on your heels to flex your thigh muscles. Hold onto the tension. Now relax and notice the difference. Repeat the exercise.
19.	Now, curl your toes downward to cause your calves to tense. Hold onto the tension. Now relax. Repeat the exercise.
20.	Now, draw your toes upward, causing your shins to feel tense. Pay attention to the tension. Now relax. Repeat the exercise.
21.	Now, scan your body. Notice if there are any tense spots. Repeat the exercise in that area.
22.	Enjoy the more relaxed feeling throughout your entire body. When you are ready, slowly return to your normal activities, holding on to that feeling of relaxation.

Exercise available at elemen.com.au

Once you have learned the technique, you can use a shorter version. You may prefer to just focus on the areas of your body that are particularly tense. It is certainly the case that some people tend to carry their muscle tension in one or two areas. Here is a shorter version that will allow you to tailor the procedure to suit your own needs.

	Relaxing using progressive muscle relaxation (short version)
1.	Choose a comfortable place where it is quiet. Lay down or sit in a comfortable position with your feet flat on the floor.
2.	Begin to work your way through groups of muscles by tensing them and relaxing them. For example, if you start with your forehead, tighten the muscles in your forehead by frowning. Hold for a few moments (10-15 seconds), then release, allowing the muscle in your forehead to relax, enjoying that experience for about 60 seconds. Notice the difference between the tension and the relaxation.
3.	Then, move on to the next group of muscles. You can work through groups of muscles from the top of your head to the tips of your toes, or you can select areas of your body that present a particular problem of tension for you.
4.	Repeat the process until you have worked your way through the groups of muscles you have selected.
5.	Repeat that process again, first tensing the muscles, holding that tension for five to ten seconds, and then relaxing those muscles.

Exercise available at elemen.com.au

So, controlling your breathing and, thus, lowering your heart rate will help you feel less anxious, as will reducing your muscle tension. However, there are other approaches you can take to anxiety management.

Quietening your mind

One of the problems with being anxious and 'revved up' is that your mind fills up with anxiety-provoking thoughts. When you have experienced abuse and, indeed, when you continue to fear the abuser, you cannot seem to stop thinking in an endless stream of anxiety-provoking thoughts. This makes it very difficult to get your nervous system back under control. The thoughts racing through your mind do not allow you to relax. So, included here are some exercises that should help you settle your mind.

The first exercises aim to teach you to self-soothe. If you can learn to settle yourself, the racing thoughts in your mind may follow. The quieter your nervous system, the less active your mind is with anxiety-provoking thoughts.

What you are aiming to do is find ways to soothe yourself. Most of us can understand how we go about soothing an upset child. We might hold and rock a distressed child and say soothing things. What you are looking for are versions of self-soothing strategies that will help you, as an adult, to alleviate your distressed state.

The goal of developing self-soothing strategies is to create for yourself some moments of less distress. The strategies are aimed at reducing your heightened state to a more manageable level. They allow your nervous system's arousal level to be brought back under your control. So, strategies that allow you to focus on the here and now are the ones that will allow you to choose to be in a quieter state with a greater sense of peace of mind.

Consider the proposed self-soothing strategies listed below and select ones that you think might assist you. These may be things you have tried before or ones you feel might work for you. Some of these strategies require you to make an effort to seek out the means of engaging with them. However, others are using things that are readily available or easily obtained.

	Self-soothing strategies
	Take a shower or a warm bath. Focus your attention on the sensations created by the water. Enjoy the feeling of the water on your skin and the warmth of the water. Turn your mind off to other thoughts and just focus on the water and its warmth.
	Play with your pet or just stroke your dog's or cat's coat. Interacting with your pet has been demonstrated to be soothing for many pet owners.
	Change into your most comfortable clothes. Enjoy the feel of the fabric and the degree of comfort you feel from wearing these items of clothing.
	Go for a swim. Enjoy the sensation of being in the water. Allow those sensations to quiet your mind. Even if you are not a good swimmer, bobbing around in the water can produce the same sensations.
	Treat yourself to a massage if that appeals to you. Allow your muscles to relax and your mind to quiet.
	Listen to soothing music. Allow your attention to be directed to the music rather than have the music in the background.
	Listen to an audiobook, even if your distress makes it difficult to concentrate. Try to pay attention to each word that is spoken. If you lose track of the story, you can always return to the previous track and pick up the story again.
	Turn on the television or talkback radio and engage in listening to what is being broadcast. The goal here is to focus your attention on the conversations as they play out rather than selecting a programme you are excited to watch or listen to. It is the process of listening to others talking that is soothing.

	Listen to the sounds of water running. Again, the aim is to listen to the sounds of the water, stopping your mind from going to other intrusive thoughts. You can find the sound of running water in various places. You can visit a naturally occurring water course or waterfall. You could listen to running water from an outdoor garden fountain. However, you can also get an indoor personal fountain that can be used at any time. Alternatively, you can listen to recorded sounds of water running.
	Find something soothing to look at. This might be by the water or an outdoor space such as a park. It could be photographs or paintings that you find soothing or relaxing. The goal is to find something to look at that is engaging for you, and that you find relaxing and soothing.

Exercise available at elemen.com.au

Building on this notion of self-soothing, it is a good idea to be more present in your focus. If you give it some consideration, you will find that the thoughts racing through your mind when you are anxious typically are not related to what is happening in the here and now. Our thoughts tend to engage in time-travelling, that is, they are focused either on what has already happened or what is to come. They rarely focus on what is happening in the present moment when you are trying to relax.

Usually, at these times, nothing is happening that is worth worrying about. If you could deliberately spend more time focused on the here and now and less time on the past or future, you would have a better chance of relaxing and quieting your overly stimulated nervous system.

The suggestion of focusing on the here and now is based on the notion of mindfulness. Mindfulness refers to your ability to be aware of your emotions, your physical state, your actions and your thoughts in a state of mind that is absent from judgment or criticism of your experience. Research has demonstrated that mindfulness helps you to control symptoms of anxiety, to control the distress caused by particular situations, to increase your capacity to relax, and to learn how to cope better with challenging situations.

Based on the notion of mindfulness, we have included some exercises you can use to quiet your mind by focusing on the here and now. To do this well, you may need to practice the skill. When you first learn these techniques, it is easy to become distracted and return to your racing thoughts. Do not worry if this happens. Just return to your exercise and continue.

Mindful listening
Sit in a comfortable place, preferably by yourself. If you wish, close your eyes.
Start to focus your attention on the sounds around you. Identify each sound.
Notice the changes in the sounds from moment to moment.
Notice the times between sounds when it is quiet.
Focus your attention both on what is happening inside and outside.
Pay attention to the sounds and nothing else. Do not make judgments about the sounds. Just acknowledge the sound then listen to the next one.
If thoughts about other things come into your mind, put them to one side then return to listening to the sounds around you.
Do this for a few minutes or until you are ready to stop.

Exercise available at elemen.com.au

Let's try another mindfulness exercise.

Mindful use of your senses	
Sight	Look around you. Allow your attention to be drawn to five things in your immediate environment that you might not normally pay any attention to. For example, this might be the way the fruit is sitting in the fruit bowl, the way your curtain is hanging, or the way your books are placed on your bookcase. Allow your attention to rest on each of these things. Keep your focus directed at the items, setting aside any other thoughts that come into your mind.
Touch	Bring your attention to four things you can feel at this moment in time. For example, it may be the feel of the sun on your skin, or the feel of the fabric of your clothes against your skin, or the feel of the chair underneath you, or the feel of the table surface where your hand is resting. Allow your attention to rest on each of these feelings. Keep your focus directed at each sense of touch, setting aside any other thoughts that come into your mind.

Hearing	Listen to the sounds in your surroundings. Notice three things you can hear. For example, you might hear the sounds of cars travelling along the road, the noise of the refrigerator, or the sound of the wind in the trees. Focus your attention on each of these sounds. If other thoughts come into your mind, let those thoughts go and return to focusing on the sounds you can hear.
Smell	Pay attention and search for two things you can smell. For example, you might be able to smell whatever you are cooking, the scent of plants in your garden, or the sea air if you live near the water. Keep your attention focused on each of these smells. If other distracting thoughts come into your mind, let these thoughts go and return to focusing on the things you can smell.
Taste	When you are eating, focus your attention on the tastes you are experiencing. For example, take a sip of your coffee and notice the taste. Bite into your sandwich and notice the flavours. Really pay attention to the flavours of the things you are tasting. If you become distracted, let go of these interfering thoughts and return to focusing on the things you are tasting.

Exercise available at elemen.com.au

And here is one last mindfulness exercise.

Mindful walking	
1.	As you are ready for your walk, stand still for a moment. Sense the weight on your feet as you stand there. Feel how your muscles are supporting you and maintaining your stability and balance. Be aware of your arms in a comfortable position of your choice (e.g., by your side or hands clasped, either at the front or at your back). Allow yourself to stand there, relaxed but alert.
2.	Begin to walk. Choose a comfortable pace, not too fast and not too slow. Pay attention to how your feet and legs feel (e.g., their heaviness or lightness, the energy, or even any pain). The way your legs and feet feel will form the focus of your attention. If you become distracted, return to focusing on your legs and feet.
3.	Pay attention to the way in which you lift your feet and place them back down on the surface on which you are walking. Notice how you lift your foot, swing your leg and place your foot down again ahead of where you were a moment before. Walk in a natural and relaxed manner. Move your arms in a way that feels normal for you.

4.	It is likely that your mind will wander as you walk along. Your attention will be drawn to what is around you or thoughts that come into your mind. Acknowledge that you have been distracted and return to focusing on the process of walking… the lifting of your foot, the swing of your leg and the placement of your foot in front of you. Just gently return your attention to the sensations of walking.
5.	You might focus on a point ahead of you. Focus on the steps you take as you move towards that point. One step at a time. Experience fully the sensations of walking.
6.	Keep walking mindfully until you reach your destination or the point where you decide to turn around and mindfully walk back to where you started.

Exercise available at elemen.com.au

These types of strategies can help deal with another manifestation of too much stress and too much anxiety, that is, sleep disturbance. Let's consider this next.

Dealing with sleep disturbance

One of the consequences of your nervous system being revved up and having too many stressful thoughts is that your sleep can become disturbed. You can become fatigued as a consequence and it becomes more difficult for you to cope with the demands of your day.

There are three types of insomnia. You might experience any one or all three of these types of sleep problems.

> *Trouble going to sleep.* This is where you are unable to go to sleep despite being tired.
>
> *Trouble staying asleep.* This is where you repeatedly wake throughout the night but, after a period of time, you are able to go back to sleep.
>
> *Waking early and being unable to go back to sleep.* This is where you wake early in the morning and, despite needing more sleep, you cannot return to sleep.

Each of these types of sleep problems is understandable if you take into consideration your stages of sleep.

Table 4: A description of the stages of sleep.

	Stages of sleep
Stage 1	This is a transitional stage from wakefulness to sleep. It is associated with very light sleep. During this stage, muscle activity slows down.
Stage 2	During this stage, your sleep starts to deepen. Your breathing pattern changes and slows as does your heart rate. Your body temperature drops slightly.
Stage 3	It is at this stage that deep sleep begins to be experienced. To signal the onset of deep sleep, your brain starts to generate slow delta waves.
Stage 4	This is when you are most deeply asleep. During this stage, your muscle activity is limited.
REM sleep	This refers to Rapid Eye Movement Sleep. It occurs when you are at the closest point to wakefulness. It is associated with vivid dreaming. During this stage, your heart rate increases.

Over the course of the night, you will cycle through these stages. For the first half or so of the night, you will cycle down into the deep sleep associated with stages 3 and 4. However, as the night progresses, the cycling pattern is lighter and does not involve deep sleep. This pattern is demonstrated in the diagram below. Periods of REM sleep occur at the point in the cycle when you are closest to waking.

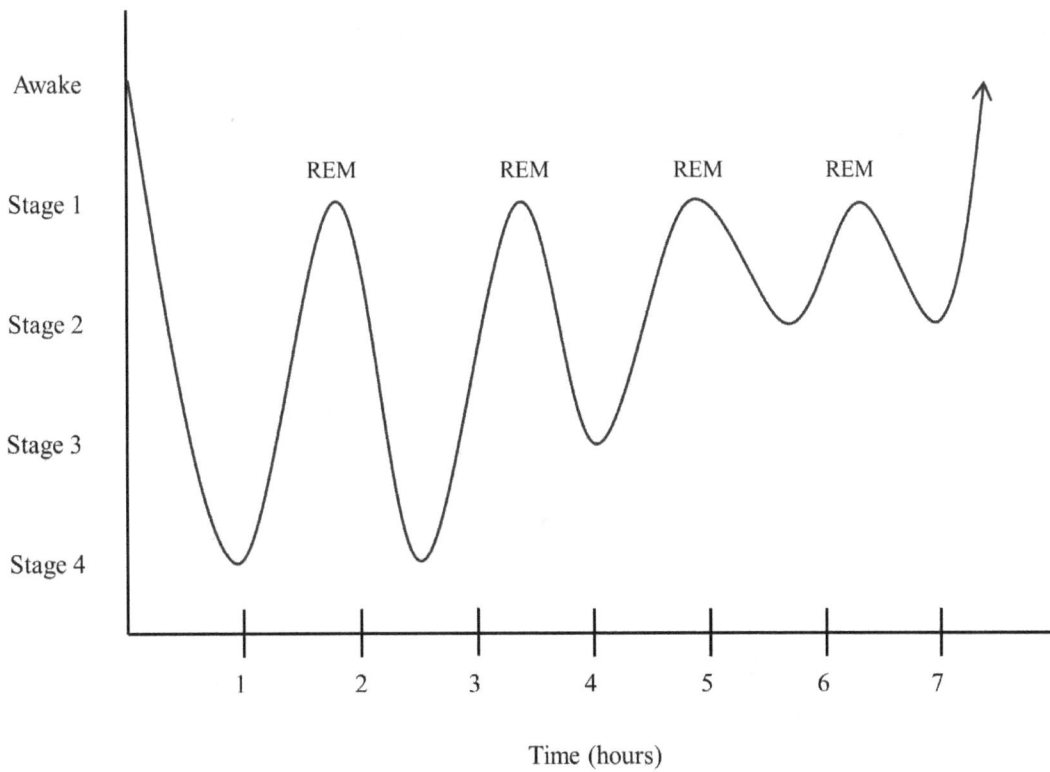

Figure 4: The cycles of sleep over the course of a sleep period.

When you have trouble falling asleep at the beginning of the night, you are struggling to enter into Stage 1 of sleep. This transitional stage is designed to pull you down into deeper sleep. Stage 1 allows you to do what your brain is inviting you to do, that is, go to sleep. Unfortunately, if you are stressed, your nervous system is generally too aroused to allow this to occur. Your nervous system fights against this natural urge to sleep. Your stressful thoughts are indicating to your brain that it is a good idea to stay awake in case something happens to which you need to respond.

When you have trouble staying asleep, you tend to wake up when your sleep cycle reaches those points where it is closest to wakefulness. In general, your nervous system is too aroused to allow you to stay asleep. Then, as soon as you wake, your mind turns to stressful thoughts that then keep you awake until you can get back to sleep. This can happen many times throughout the night.

When you are troubled by waking early and being unable to return to sleep, this usually occurs in the second part of the night when you have moved past the deep sleep cycles. Your sleep is lighter, and when your nervous system is too aroused, and you come close to wakefulness, you become completely awake, your stressful thoughts begin, and you cannot get back to sleep.

What can I do about my sleep problems?

Each of these types of sleep disturbance can be influenced by racing thoughts. These thoughts are usually of a stressful nature. They increase your nervous system arousal, making it difficult to get any rest.

Here is a series of simple steps that can help you have a better night's sleep.

	Simple sleep strategy
1.	In the evening, avoid caffeine and sugary drinks and food.
2.	In the lead-up to your bedtime, start to wind down. Turn off stimulating television or stop engaging in other activities around the house that cause you to feel more alert.
3.	Have a small snack rich in carbohydrates.
4.	Get into a comfortable bed and into a comfortable position. Slow your breathing. Relax your muscle tension.
5.	Give your mind something to think about that is not emotionally arousing. This could be writing a simple story in your head or listing in your mind all the countries you can think of, starting with A, then B, etc. Alternatively, count backwards by 7s from a randomly selected number.
6.	If your thoughts drift to more stressful thoughts, acknowledge that is what is happening then return to the activity you chose to keep your mind focused.
7.	Allow yourself to drift off to sleep.

Exercise available at elemen.com.au

The goal here is to create the right sort of internal environment to facilitate a good night's sleep. Avoid caffeine and sugary food or drinks because they can have a stimulating effect on your nervous system. In general, you should be aiming to 'turn off' by reducing the number of external stimulating activities. You do these things in preparation for sleep.

Carbohydrates can also increase your readiness for sleep. This is because carbohydrates contribute to an increase in your brain of a protein called tryptophan. This is a building block for a neurotransmitter called serotonin and a hormone called melatonin. Serotonin has a role in controlling sleep, appetite and mood. Melatonin release is triggered by darkness, and this hormone helps promote a regular sleep-wake cycle. This process, encouraged by eating a carbohydrate-rich snack before bedtime, helps you sleep.

When your mind is already overrun by thoughts that are keeping you awake, it seems counterintuitive to give your brain something else to think about. However, it is not the thoughts themselves that will keep you awake. It is the nature of the thoughts that will have an effect on your sleep. In this way, you want to distract yourself from thinking stress-related thoughts, replacing them with thoughts that will not cause you to react emotionally. You should aim to keep your brain busy with mundane thoughts so that your mind is distracted from the stress-inducing thoughts. We like to refer to this activity as 'busy work' for your brain. It is the modern-day equivalent of counting sheep.

Mundane thoughts will allow you to drift off to sleep whereas stress-related thoughts will keep you alert and awake. Your brain is always active so it is not possible to stop thinking altogether. When you think of things that cause your nervous system to respond by increasing your arousal, you will have trouble sleeping. If you think calming or even boring thoughts, your brain will trigger the processes that lead you to falling asleep.

The same strategy of giving your mind something other than stressful things to think about can be applied if you awaken during the night. Simply get settled and focus on the mundane thoughts you have selected, allowing yourself to drift off back to sleep.

As an overall strategy to allow yourself to feel more settled, it is necessary to learn to regulate your emotional state. We will consider how to do this next.

Regulating your emotions

Experiencing a stressful time, such as would occur when you leave an abusive relationship, can result in a period of strong, volatile and variable emotions. This is a difficult and uncomfortable time. Although it is quite normal to have this type of reaction, and you cannot really avoid it altogether, the aim should be to reduce the severity of your distress and shorten the duration of this challenging period if you can do so.

This does not mean that you should fight against the emotions you feel. You cannot start a war with your emotional state and expect to be the victor. You cannot ignore your emotions and expect them to just disappear. The aim should be to recognise and validate your emotional reactions, but do what you can to avoid your emotional distress escalating.

One way to do this is to focus your attention and coping efforts on your presenting emotional state. For example, if you feel anxious then give this emotion your attention and work on ways to cope with your anxiety. The anxiety you are feeling is your primary emotion at that time. It is the emotion you feel directly because of what has happened to you.

It sounds straightforward. However, human beings are complex creatures who have the capacity to make themselves feel even more miserable. We experience different secondary emotions as a result of our reaction to the primary emotion. Let's consider how this might work with your anxious feelings in the aftermath of the end of the abusive relationship.

What happened?	*I left an abusive relationship.*
How do you feel?	*I feel anxious* (primary emotion).
How do you react to the anxiety?	*I don't like feeling anxious, and I want it to go away.*
What do you say to yourself?	*"I hate feeling anxious."* *"I should be able to control this feeling."*
What do you feel then?	*I feel self-critical* (secondary emotion).
How do you react to this feeling?	*I don't like the feeling, and I want it to go away.*
What do you say to yourself?	*"Here I am blaming myself."* *"I am just making things worse for myself."*

What do you feel then?	*I feel annoyed* (secondary emotion).
How do you react to this feeling?	*I feel uncomfortable and stressed.*
What do you say to yourself?	*"I am feeling so bad I will never get over this."*
What do you feel then?	*I feel despairing* (secondary emotion).

So now, instead of only feeling anxious, you feel anxious, self-critical, annoyed and despairing. Your primary emotion of anxiety was directly related to the problem situation that triggered the emotional reaction. The secondary emotions of self-criticism, annoyance and despair all developed as a result of your reaction to the primary emotion, that is, your anxiety.

Your emotional reactions can be difficult to manage because what started as a straightforward emotional response to a stressful event turns into a confusing array of emotions. Sometimes, these emotions can compete with each other and pull you in different directions. For example, you can feel both sad and angry or angry and excited. Trying to deal with one of these emotions can be undermined by your efforts to deal with the other emotion.

There is a need to simplify things when you are dealing with difficult life events. You can learn to focus on your primary emotions as they arise and adopt strategies to deal with them. Let's start by looking at a way to identify your emotions so you know to what you should be giving your attention.

Recognising and dealing with your emotions

Let's start by taking the process of experiencing an emotional reaction a step at a time.

What happened?

Here, consider the situation that developed that resulted in you feeling these strong emotions. Identify specific details of what happened rather than talking in generalised terms (e.g., "I never cope", "I always make mistakes").

Why did this situation occur?

Consider the possible causes of the problem situation. This is an important step. It gives you the opportunity to interpret the meaning of the problem situation in an effort to help you understand why you are feeling the strong emotions you are experiencing.

How were you feeling as a result of this situation?

Try to identify your primary emotional response to the situation and then consider the secondary emotions you experience as well.

What is it that you wanted to do *as a result of how you were feeling?*

Here we are referring to the urges or impulses you have to act in response to the emotional state you are in. When feeling strong emotions, people tend to experience urges to do more extreme actions.

It does not follow that you will always do these things, however, thoughts about doing them can be present. It is worth noting that people tend to *think* about doing extreme things much more often than they ever *do* them. What this means is that you control the impulse to act in a 'over the top' way. If you can control these impulses, you can control others in a way that will allow you to have a more settled and reasonable response to provoking situations.

What did you actually do *and* say?

Here, you are considering what you actually did rather than what you had an urge to do.

After experiencing those emotions and actions, how did they affect you?

Here, we are referring to the consequences for you of experiencing those strong emotional states and your reactions to those states by choosing to act in a particular way.

To try and make sense of what you are feeling and why you are feeling it, we suggest you use the worksheet below. It is designed to help you understand how you are reacting to the problems you are facing, and this may direct you to how you can cope with the situation. First, let's look at how you can use this worksheet.

Understanding your emotions worksheet - example
Time and date: *Thursday 10th*
What happened? *I was home alone, and I started to feel really anxious. I paced around, and I couldn't settle.*
Why did this situation occur? *I had shut myself off from everyone for days. By Thursday, I hadn't spoken to anyone, and I had only my own thoughts for company.*
How were you feeling as a result of that situation? *I realised I was really alone and that was unsettling. In reaction to that, I felt anxious, and I couldn't settle down.*
What is it that you wanted to do as a result of how you were feeling? *I wanted the anxiety to stop, so I thought about calling my ex-partner and asking if she would take me back. That seemed to be a better option than the anxiety I was feeling.*
What did you actually do and say? *I turned on the television and watched it for a while, and then I went to bed.*
After experiencing those emotions and actions, how did they affect you? *I felt empty and alone. The bad anxiety passed, but I still felt empty.*

Here is the worksheet you can use.

Understanding your emotions worksheet
Time and date:
What happened?
Why did this situation occur?
How were you feeling as a result of this situation?
What is it that you wanted to do as a result of how you were feeling?
What did you actually do and say?
After experiencing those emotions and actions, how did they affect you?

Worksheet available at elemen.com.au

The link between your emotions and your behaviour

It is worthwhile to understand the link between your emotional state and the things you choose to do in response to that emotion. This is important. It is difficult to control your behaviour choices if you do not appreciate the link between how you feel and what you do.

Let's consider how you might behave in relation to your emotional responses. Consider this example.

I felt	What I did
Anxious	*I shut myself off from everyone. I paced around at home day and night.*

Understanding this link between your emotional state and your behaviour can help you learn to make different choices in how you act when you are upset. We will explore this further when we consider building your coping strategies, but let's consider here how you might opt to do different things. Consider the same example but now let's look at how this person might have chosen to do things differently.

I felt	What I did	What I could have done instead
Anxious	*I shut myself off from everyone. I paced around at home day and night.*	*I could have reached out to my family for support. I could have contacted a counselling service.*

Let's take this one step further and consider the likely outcomes of the initial behaviour choice and the alternative one.

I felt…	*Anxious*
I did…	*I shut myself off from everyone. I paced around at home day and night.*
What happened?	*I just felt worse and worse.*
A better choice…	*I could have reached out to my family for support. I could have contacted a counselling service.*
Likely outcome…	*I would have felt better much sooner. I know my family would support me and would offer to comfort me. They would likely come around and be with me so I wouldn't feel so anxious and alone. If I contacted a counselling service, I would have received some good advice about how to manage my anxiety.*

Initially, you can work on thinking up alternative and healthier behaviours after the event. This will allow you to learn how to make better choices by considering the different outcomes of various behaviours. It will then become easier to apply this strategy when you feel the emotional reaction so that you can choose the better behaviour at the time and avoid doing things that might feel all right at the time but do not help you in the longer term. Below is a worksheet you can use.

The emotion-behaviour link worksheet	
I feel/felt…	
I did/I felt the urge to do…	
What happened/ what would have happened?	
A better choice…	

Likely outcome…	

Worksheet available at elemen.com.au

Here, you have learned to identify your emotional reactions and to respond to them differently, focusing on your primary emotions and responding to your urges to act in a different way. Now we need to focus on building your coping skills so that you can choose to do particular things that will help you overcome difficult times.

Learn to cope

The fact that you will have a strong and seemingly overwhelming emotional response to the end of the abusive relationship you experienced and the fact that you had experienced those abusive episodes requires that you look for ways to cope. That is what we do when we are faced with problem situations in our lives… we try to use the skills we have to cope with our problems.

We all have our own coping resources and individual coping skills. Coping resources are the things we have available to us to help us cope, such as family and friends. Coping skills are the strategies we are good at that we use to deal with the problems we face. We have our own particular coping resources and specific coping skills because there is not one particular way of coping.

In a general sense, the way you will cope with this experience will likely be a reflection of the way you have dealt with and solved other problems throughout your life. That is, the way you cope will reflect your general style of coping.

Your goal should be to understand how you cope and to make good use of the coping resources you have or can create, as well as the particular coping skills you have developed or can develop. This is true even if you take into account the fact that what you are experiencing at the moment may be a more challenging problem than other problems you have dealt with in your life. For those of you who feel you do not cope well with life problems, it may be the case you have been trying to develop coping skills based on a pattern of coping skills that does not suit you.

To understand the way you cope and to use this knowledge to choose the best strategies to cope with the end of the abusive relationship and to promote your recovery from the experiences you have had, consideration needs to be given to the fundamental differences people can have in the way they approach problem situations. Let's consider the different approaches to coping so that you can work out your own preferred coping style.

Problem-focused coping vs. emotion-focused coping

To start, a distinction can be made between problem-focused coping strategies and emotion-focused strategies.

Who are problem-focused copers?

Problem-focused copers deal with their problems by considering the problem situation. They tend to want to *do* something when they are confronted with a problem. They are most comfortable when there are specific things related to the problem that can be the focus of their attention. These people just want to *do* something to fix the problem.

Who are emotion-focused copers?

Emotion-focused copers are the people who deal with their problems by expressing their emotional reactions to the situation. They will talk about the problem and cry when they feel the need. They see the value of looking to others to share their feelings about their problem. In the context of the situation they are facing, the emotion-focused coper will say "I need to talk about how I am feeling".

Are people either emotion-focused or problem-focused copers?

Some people are strongly problem-focused copers, and some people are strongly emotion-focused copers. Others fall somewhere on the continuum between the two extreme positions. You may be more problem-focused than emotion-focused in your coping but still make use of some emotion-focused strategies… or the reverse.

You will be able to do a little exercise to find your coping preferences or to confirm them if you already have a good idea of where on the continuum you fall. But, first, we have to consider one other element.

Problem-approach vs. problem-avoidance coping

People assume that if we talk about coping strategies, they have to be good ones that will help us deal with the problems we face. This is not the case. People's coping style can be divided on the basis of whether they tend to front up to their problems or whether they prefer to avoid them. This is the case for both problem-focused copers and emotion-focused copers.

Let's start by looking at problem-focused coping. How would problem approach and problem avoidance strategies differ? Consider the examples in the table below.

Table 5: Examples of problem-focused approach and avoidance strategies.

Problem-focused approach strategies	Problem-focused avoidance strategies
Problem solving Problem solving coping strategies involve: Examining the problem Generating potential solutions Evaluating the likelihood of a successful outcome Moving forward and applying the strategy	*Problem avoidance* Problem avoidance coping strategies involve: Deliberately avoiding thinking about the problem Deliberately avoiding reminders of the problem
Cognitive restructuring Cognitive restructuring coping strategies involve: Reframing your thoughts to think more reasonably about the problem Correcting errors in thinking that are barriers to coping with the problem	*Wishful thinking* Wishful thinking as a coping strategy involves: Wishing the problem would go away Indulging in thoughts that things will just return to 'normal' Spending time thinking about how things will work out in your favour and as you wish

With regard to your having to deal with the aftermath of an abusive relationship, effective, problem-focused approach coping strategies may help in the following ways. They may help you think clearly about what needs to be done to resolve the situation you are facing. They can keep you focused on what you need to do without being overwhelmed by strong emotions. They can help you feel more in control.

Now, let's consider emotion-focused coping. The table below details examples of approach and avoidance emotion-focused coping strategies.

Table 6: Examples of emotion-focused approach and avoidance strategies.

Emotion-focused approach strategies	Emotion-focused avoidance strategies
Emotional expression Emotional expression as a coping strategy involves: Being open and talking about how you are feeling Allowing yourself to experience your emotional reactions in relation to the problem Using emotional expression as a form of catharsis, letting off steam to allow yourself to feel better for a while	*Self-criticism* Self-criticism as a coping strategy involves: Blaming yourself for the problem Criticising yourself for failing to control your emotional reaction to the problem Viewing yourself as more generally deficient than is warranted
Social support Using social support as a coping strategy involves: Turning to family and friends for support Talking with your support network about how you are feeling Taking comfort from your support people Allowing your support network to offer instrumental support/practical help	*Social withdrawal* Social withdrawal as a copy strategy involves: Cutting yourself off from family and friends Failing to seek professional support when it is needed Refusing assistance offered by the people who wish to help you or would be willing to do so

When we consider you having to deal with the aftermath of an abusive relationship, the effective emotion-focused approach coping strategies may be of assistance to you in the following ways. They can help you feel some relief when you feel overwhelmed by emotion. They can help you take advantage of your support network of family and friends. They can help you deal with the emotional roller coaster ride of emotions that you experience with this stressful life event.

Identifying your preferred coping style

The goal here is to identify the type of coping that works best for you. If you are an emotion-focused coper, you may see the value of a problem-focused coping approach, but it is unlikely that you could comfortably adopt problem-focused coping strategies and expect them to work for you. Your efforts would be better directed at taking advantage of your preferred style of coping and using problem-approach strategies.

Here is an exercise in determining what type of coping style best characterises your preferred type. Tick the boxes if you typically use the listed coping strategy.

	How do I normally cope?
Problem solving	
	I work on finding ways to solve the problems I face.
	I work out what I should do, and then I follow the plan.
	I like to work out a plan and then move forward.
	I believe there is a solution to every problem.
Problem avoidance	
	I try to act like nothing is wrong.
	When faced with a problem, I choose not to do anything, even when I know I should.
	I try not to spend any time thinking about the problem.
	When the problem comes to mind, I push it out of my head.
Cognitive restructuring	
	I think about my problems in a way that allows me to realise I can manage them.
	I think about the problem to change the way I react to it.
	I try to look on the bright side of any situation.
	I try to put things into perspective.

Wishful thinking	
	When faced with a problem, I just wish it would go away.
	I just hope a miracle will happen to make everything all right.
	I hope the problem will fix itself.
	I wish that someone would come and fix the problem for me.
Emotion expression	
	When faced with a problem, I allow myself to express my feelings about it.
	I do not try to bottle up my feelings; I let them go so that I can feel better.
	I do not hide my feelings about the problem from other people.
	When faced with a problem, I just need some time to experience my feelings.
Self-criticism	
	I blame myself for the problem I am facing.
	I ask myself what I have done to make the problem happen.
	I tend to hold myself responsible for the problems I face.
	When a problem occurs, I feel I should have done things differently.
Social support	
	I turn to the people I know will listen when I talk about how I feel.
	I feel better when I can talk to others about my problems.
	When faced with a problem, I seek advice from people I trust.
	I allow other people to offer help and support when I am dealing with a problem.

	Social withdrawal
	When faced with a problem, I like to avoid other people and spend time by myself.
	When I am struggling with a problem, I do not want to be around other people.
	I do not share my thoughts and feelings with others.
	I do not accept the help others offer.

Checklist available at elemen.com.au

What type of coper are you? Add up the ticks you have placed in each of the categories and enter the number in the following table.

Ways of coping worksheet	
Problem-focused strategies	*Emotion-focused strategies*
_____ Problem-solving _____ Cognitive restructuring _____ Problem avoidance _____ Wishful thinking _____ Total	_____ Emotion expression _____ Social support _____ Self-criticism _____ Social withdrawal _____ Total
Problem-approach strategies	*Problem-avoidance strategies*
_____ Problem-solving _____ Cognitive restructuring _____ Emotion expression _____ Social support _____ Total	_____ Problem-avoidance _____ Wishful thinking _____ Self-criticism _____ Social withdrawal _____ Total

Score sheet available at elemen.com.au

When comparing your problem-focused and emotion-focused strategies, see where you have scored the highest. This may show a strong preference for one type of coping strategy or the other. If so, you can build on your preferred coping type when you consider what coping strategies will help you with your current situation. If you have similar totals for both problem-focused and emotion-focused strategies, you would do best to include each type in your coping plan.

When considering whether you use problem-approach strategies or problem-avoidance strategies, you are considering whether adjustments have to be made in the way you cope. If you predominantly use problem-avoidance strategies, you can learn to abandon those in favour of problem-approach strategies while staying within the same style of coping strategy, that is, problem-focused or emotion-focused.

We are now going to consider how to take full advantage of your ways of coping, building on problem-approach strategies and letting go of problem-avoidance strategies.

Building your coping repertoire

As you now better understand the ways you cope, you can start to build a plan of how you are going to move forward, adopting coping strategies that work for you. Let's consider some examples of coping strategies you could adopt.

Problem-focused strategies

We will start by looking at problem-solving strategies. Here you are trying to work out a plan of how you would go about solving a specific problem situation, followed by decision-making with regard to which potential solution you would choose. You then should be able to follow through and move towards solving your problem.

Let's consider an example of this process.

Example of a problem-solving strategy

What is the problem? Clearly define the problem you are facing.

My former partner is either driving past where I am living or parking across the street from the house with the intention of harassing me.

Generate as many possible solutions as you can. List the ones that are likely to work.

I could do the following:

> *I could do nothing and hope she goes away.*
>
> *I could contact her and ask her to stay away from my home.*
>
> *I could go and stay with friends or family until things blow over.*
>
> *I could seek a restraining order, preventing her from coming near my home or me.*

Consider the likelihood of each of these strategies being successful.

The likely outcomes are:

If I did nothing, I doubt things would change. Throughout our relationship, she persevered with harassing and intimidating behaviours for long periods of time... sometimes months. Also, if she thinks she has gotten away with intimidating me, it is likely that her behaviour will escalate.

By contacting her, I would be opening up a means of dialogue that I do not wish to have. In addition, she would learn that what she was doing was having a negative effect on me and I was giving her the power to control me and the degree of upset I experience. This is likely to embolden her to act even more intrusively.

If I go and stay with friends or family, I could not guarantee that things would blow over. Also, even if she does not know where I am staying, this is really only a temporary solution. I would have to return to my home at some point. Further, I would be concerned that she would find out where I was staying and would then harass my friends or family members putting them at risk of harm.

If I sought a restraining order, I could more comfortably stay in my own home. If she breached the order, I could easily get support from the police. Also, by doing this, I would demonstrate to her that I am now willing to stand up to her, letting her know that I will not tolerate her tactics any longer.

Select the problem-solving strategy that is likely to work the best. *I think I will seek a restraining order. I have enough evidence of her abuse, and I have photographic evidence of her current harassment, so I feel that there is a good likelihood that I will be successful. This is likely to send a strong message that I will not passively tolerate her behaviour any longer.*
What are you going to do next? *I am going to access the application form for a restraining order online. I will complete the application and submit it to the court as soon as possible. If needed, I will seek legal advice and support to obtain the order.*

In this example, the person has thought about the problem and identified possible options for resolving it. The person then considered what the likely outcome for each possible solution would be. They then chose their preferred solution and worked out a plan for their next step. This is a good problem-solving approach.

Here is a problem-solving worksheet you can use.

Problem-solving strategy worksheet
What is the problem? Clearly define the problem you are facing.
Generate as many possible solutions as you can. List the ones that are likely to work.
Consider the likelihood of each of these strategies being successful.

Select the problem-solving strategy that is likely to work the best.
What are you going to do next?

Worksheet available at elemen.com.au

Now, let's consider a cognitive restructuring approach to coping. Remember, cognitive restructuring refers to you changing the way you view a situation and think about it so that you can achieve a better perspective. Below is an example of a cognitive restructuring approach to addressing a problem situation.

Example of a cognitive restructuring strategy
What is the problem? *My former partner sent me a message saying that she intended to take the children from me and have them live with her. She said she would 'see me in court'. So, my problem is that she is going to the Family Court to apply for the children to be in her care.*
What am I thinking? *I am going to lose my children. They will end up living with their abusive mother, and she will take her anger out on them. I won't be able to protect them.*
What evidence do I have that this is true? *Well… she said she was going to do this but I guess that isn't evidence it will happen.*
What evidence do I have against this being true? *She has a long history of claiming she was going to do things that she did not end up doing. She does not have the financial means to do this. She has shown no indication of actually wanting the children in her care.*

> Even if it was true, what is the worst thing that would happen?
>
> *Even if she did make an application to the Family Court, I have ample evidence of her abuse and the danger she presents to the children to make a strong case for the children remaining in my care. I have lots of people who support me and know of her behaviour, including her own parents and sister. She has a police record, and her abusive behaviour is known to the police, the courts and child protective services. So, the worst thing that would happen is likely to be having to go through a legal process, but there is every indication the children would remain with me.*

> What is my conclusion?
>
> *I believe this is just another attempt to intimidate me and make me fearful. I think I can successfully deal with this if she does make an application to the Family Court but, in the meantime, I think I will focus on other things I can do something about.*

Here, the person in this example challenged the way he was thinking about his situation. He examined whether the situation was as bad as he was interpreting it to be. Having realised that was not the case, he then worked out a better and more realistic way of thinking about his problem. You can see that his alternative thoughts about his situation would make it easier for him to cope. He had been tormented by thoughts that the children would be taken away from him. Instead, by working through the situation, he was able to see that he had overreacted to the type of intimidating behaviour his former partner typically used to upset him.

Below is a worksheet you can use to consider a cognitive restructuring coping strategy.

Cognitive restructuring strategy worksheet
What is the problem?
What am I thinking?
What evidence do I have that this is true?
What evidence do I have against this being true?
Even if it was true, what is the worst thing that would happen?
What is my conclusion?

Worksheet available at elemen.com.au

Emotion-focused strategies

Next, we will consider how to enhance your emotional expression coping skills.

Example of an emotion expression strategy
What is the problem? *I didn't want people to know how badly I had been abused by my former partner.*
What did I do? *I chose not to tell my family about what had happened to me or how I was feeling, and I tried to cope on my own.*
What were the advantages of doing this? *None, really. I suppose I am protecting my privacy but it doesn't seem to be working for me.*
What were the disadvantages of doing this? *I couldn't talk about how I was feeling even if I wanted to. I couldn't talk to someone and just let my bottled-up feelings go. I have been pretending that everything is okay, and that has been really hard, hiding how I have been feeling. There have been times when I have felt so anxious I didn't think I could cope, and there was no one to turn to for help.*
What could I have done differently? *I could have told my family what has happened but told them there might be times when I wanted to talk about it but times when I didn't want to talk.*
What would the advantages have been of doing things this other way? *I would have felt like I wasn't carrying around this huge secret so I would have felt relieved. I would have had family available to talk to about how I was feeling when things were too much for me to cope with. This would have allowed me the opportunity to express how I was feeling in a genuine way. I could have got the sympathy and understanding that I needed. My family would have found ways to help me.*
Would there have been any disadvantage of doing things this other way? *Not really. People would know about my relationship, but I see now that it wouldn't be a disadvantage because it would allow me to talk openly about how I was feeling.*

> What will I do next time I feel like this?
>
> *I will just sit my family down and tell them what has happened and why I feel so anxious. I will ask for their support, which I know I will receive. I will call them when I feel anxious and need to talk about how I am feeling.*

In this case, the person went through a process of examining the pros and cons associated with the decision he made to not tell anyone about what happened during the relationship. He recognised that this had prevented him from genuinely expressing his emotions in a way that would have been a relief for him. The conclusion was reached that the better option was to allow himself to react in a genuine way to what he was feeling by telling people what had happened so that he did not have to pretend to be all right when he did not feel that way.

Below is a worksheet you can use to develop emotion expression coping strategies.

Emotion expression strategy worksheet
What is the problem?
What did I do?
What were the advantages of doing this?
What were the disadvantages of doing this?
What could I have done differently?

What would the advantages have been of doing things this other way?
Would there have been any disadvantages of doing things this other way?
What will I do next time I feel like this?

Worksheet available at elemen.com.au

Finally, we can consider how to use social support as a coping strategy.

Example of social support as a strategy
What is the problem? *There have been times when I have felt so anxious that I believed I could not look after myself properly. I felt I couldn't make important decisions because I felt so anxious. There have been many times when I couldn't do normal daily things like shopping and cooking for myself.*
What have I done in response to this problem? *I just hid out at home and ignored my own needs. I have just suffered by myself.*
How has responding in this way helped me with my problem? *It hasn't helped at all. The decisions I have to make don't get made. My shopping doesn't get done. I don't eat.*
What could I do instead? *I could just ask my family to help me. I could ask them to help work through the decisions I have to make. I could ask them to help me look after myself until I am able to do it for myself.*

How would this be likely to work out?
I know my family would rush to help. I trust their advice, and I know they can help me with the decisions I have to make. I know they would look after me if they knew I needed them to do that.
So, what am I going to do next?
Next time I feel like I can't cope, I will pick up the phone and call my family. I will tell them how badly I am feeling and ask them to come to my assistance.

Here, the person thought through his situation and realised he was doing the opposite of what he should have been doing to fix his problems. He realised the solution was available to him and there were advantages to pursuing the solution. It was an easy step then to follow through with his plan and reach out to others.

Below is a worksheet for you to use with a social support coping strategy.

Social support strategy worksheet
What is the problem?
What have I done in response to this problem?
What could I do instead?
How would this be likely to work out?
So, what am I going to do next?

Worksheet available at elemen.com.au

In moving forward, remember to choose the coping strategies that best suit your preferred coping style. Always choose approach strategies rather than avoidance strategies, no matter what your coping style.

Fix your thinking

It is a fact that the way we think affects how we feel and the choices we make in terms of our behaviour. Also, it is a fact that experiences such as an abusive relationship can influence the way we think, leading to us making errors in our thinking. You are going to learn more about your thinking in the coming section. Also, we will teach you to challenge those errors in thinking so that you can feel better and behave differently.

How are our thoughts affected?

As we go through life, we can develop unhelpful thinking styles or errors in our thinking. These errors influence how we interpret the world around us and how we fit into that world. In an attempt to make sense of the world, we develop 'templates' or models of how we think things should work or do work.

For example, you might develop a template that tells you that to be a worthwhile person, everyone should like you. On the surface, this seems workable. It is nice when people like you, and it makes you feel good, including your feelings about yourself. However, if you have a template that you are worthwhile *only* if everyone likes you, what happens if, for some reason, someone chooses not to like you? You then become upset about something that really is an ordinary enough experience. You then feel like you are not worthwhile, even in situations where the fact that the other person does not like you says more about them than it does about you. We have found that people choose not to like others for the oddest of reasons. For example, one person disclosed that they found they could not like people who even vaguely looked like a cousin they did not admire. Should your feelings of self-worth be affected by the fact that you look somewhat like a person you have never met? It is obvious that the answer is no. Unfortunately, your template might tell you that to be a worthwhile person, *everyone* has to like you and here is someone who does not like you. You can see the problem.

Our individual templates are put together based on information from a variety of sources, including, for example, our personality and our experiences throughout life. If the messages we receive from our experiences in life are good and healthy ones, we tend to have good and healthy templates of how the world works and how we fit into that world. However, if the messages are distorted in some way (e.g., being told you have to be the best at everything you do, that no one will like you if you disagree with them, your needs are not as important as other people's needs), then the template we develop will reflect these messages and will be unhelpful.

Core beliefs

So, how does this template affect us? It tells us how we should respond when dealing with our world and the people in it. The information we gather determines our 'core beliefs' about three things:

> How safe or dangerous we perceive the world to be.
>
> Our place in that world and our value as a person.
>
> How certain the future feels.

These core beliefs are not the 'truth' of things. They develop as a result of the information we gather along the way in life, whether or not that information is helpful or unhelpful, clear or confusing, or accurate or distorted.

If we have helpful, clear and accurate templates, then our core beliefs are healthy, and our thinking does not contain errors about how the world works and how we fit into that world. However, if we have unhelpful, confusing and distorted templates, our thinking contains errors that affect how we react to the world and how we view ourselves in that world.

Cognitive errors

Cognitive errors are the errors in thinking that occur when our templates of how the world works and how we fit into that world send us the wrong message. Our thinking about our experiences is then altered by the wrong message. For example, if an abusive partner repeatedly tells you that you are worthless, your thinking changes so that you come to believe you have no value as a person.

Problems arise when we engage in certain types of cognitive errors. Below are some of the most common cognitive errors. As you read through them, think about whether these types of errors occur in your thinking.

Table 7: Descriptions of the common errors in thinking.

\	Types of errors in thinking
Error type	*Error in thinking*
Filtering	A person whose thinking is affected by filtering takes the negative details of an event and exaggerates them while filtering out any positive aspects about the situation. For example, an abused person may focus on a mistake they made that resulted in criticism from their abusive partner, ignoring all the times they did not make a mistake and all the times others had been happy with what they had done in various ways.

Polarised thinking	With polarised thinking, things are either 'black or white' or 'all or nothing'. People who think this way place situations in 'either/or' categories, with no middle ground to account for the complexity of most situations. For example, an abused person may come to believe that either they are a good partner who can make their abuser happy or they are a terrible partner who no one would ever want.
Overgeneralisation	A person makes a conclusion based on one event or a single piece of information. In this way, if something bad happens to them on one occasion, they expect it to happen over and over again. For example, an abused person may believe that because they made a poor choice of partner once, they will make similarly poor choices again and again in the future.
Jumping to conclusions	If a person jumps to conclusions, they 'know' what the other person is thinking about without that person saying so. For example, an abused person may think others think he should have been able to handle the abuse despite them never saying such a thing.
Catastrophising	A person who catastrophises expects disaster to strike, no matter what. A person hears about a problem and uses *what-if* questions to imagine the worst outcome. For example, an abused person may believe that everyone will turn against them if he discloses the abuse he experienced.
Personalisation	A person believes that everything others do or say is some kind of direct, personal reaction to them. They take everything personally. For example, an abused person may believe that the abuser only behaved in an abusive manner because of their own shortcomings and not because the abuser had problems.
Control fallacies	This occurs when a person strongly endorses the view that there must be in control of all situations. This can occur in two ways. Firstly, there is external control where the person feels they are a helpless victim of fate or, secondly, internal control where a person assumes responsibility for the pain and unhappiness of others. For example, an abused person may believe that they have triggered the abusive behaviour in their former partner and the abuse was their fault as a consequence.

Fallacy of fairness	A person who believes they know what is fair will feel resentful and unhappy if others disagree with them. People who judge every event in their lives in terms of whether or not it is fair will often feel resentful, angry and hopeless. For example, an abused person may think that the world is unfair because they have had to endure the abuse rather than seeing that a person's poor behaviour is unrelated to any concept of a 'fair' world.
Blaming	This person holds other people responsible for their own emotional pain. Alternatively, they may blame themselves for every problem – even those clearly outside their control. For example, despite the abuse they endured being related to the abuser's behaviour choices and problems, the abused person will blame himself for the abusive episodes.
Shoulds	Should statements (e.g., I should visit my parents more) are made by people who hold rigid rules about how the world should work and how everyone should behave. Breaking these rules makes a person angry. They also feel guilty when they violate their own rules. For example, the most common manifestations of this error in thinking among abused people are the belief that they should have known from the outset that their partner was abusive and the belief that they should have done something differently to prevent the abuse.
Emotional reasoning	People with this distortion in thinking are guided by what they 'feel' is the truth. They will rely on their feelings to establish whether or not something is 'fact'. If a person feels stupid and boring, then they must be stupid and boring. Emotional reasoning blocks rationality and logic. For example, an abused person may feel worthless and of little value so they believe they are worthless and of little value.
Fallacy of change	A person with this type of thinking will believe that if they apply enough pressure, others will change to meet their needs. This person needs others to change because they cannot cope if others disagree with them or behave in ways that are contrary to how this person feels they should behave. For example, an abused person may believe that if they tried hard enough, they could have changed their partner and turned them into a non-abusive person.

Global labelling	A person generalises a small number of features or characteristics of themselves or others and inflates them into a global statement or judgment. This goes beyond overgeneralising. Rather than take into account the context of a situation, the person will apply this judgment to all aspects of a person or situation. For example, an abused person may come to view themselves as unworthy of love and unworthy of respectful treatment because they have experienced one abusive relationship.
Always being right	When a person engages in this error of thinking, they insist that all views held by them or actions done by them are correct. In their view, they cannot make a mistake or be misinformed. For example, an abused person may disbelieve supporters' acts of support or statements of sympathy and will push these people away to prove they are right that even well-meaning people are untrustworthy.
Heaven's reward fallacy	A person who engages in this type of thinking believes that a person's hard work and sacrifice will pay off in the end, as if someone is keeping track of what everyone does in life. Sharing some similarities with the fallacy of fairness thinking, this person believes that the one who does the most or, works the hardest or sacrifices the most will be the person who is rewarded at some point in the future. For example, throughout an abusive relationship, an abused person may think that if they just do the right thing, put up with the abuse and do everything they can to make the relationship work, it will pay off in the end, and their partner will change into a better person.

Let's consider how these errors in thinking affect a person's point of view. Below are examples of these types of logical errors in thinking, along with a more rational point of view.

Table 8: Examples of rational and irrational perspectives for each error in thinking.

Correcting your thinking	
Error in thinking	*A rational view*
Filtering	
Joel's family and friends told him he was doing a good job getting his life back on track. They pointed out that he was doing better than they believed they would do in similar circumstances. One person close to Joel also said that he was 'crazy' to have stayed in an abusive relationship for so long. Joel only focused on this one negative comment. He concluded that all people viewed him as crazy. This made Joel feel disheartened.	In general, Joel should be reassured that people understood his struggles well enough to see that the progress he was making in getting his life back on track was good. He could choose to understand the 'crazy' comment as a reflection of that person's understanding of the severity of the abuse he endured and how difficult it must have been for him. It would have been appropriate for Joel to consider what people were saying to him and conclude that they genuinely thought he was doing a good job in getting his life back on track.
Polarised thinking	
Stuart, in an effort to move on with his life, was studying at his local college. Overall, he was doing well with his carpentry course. However, he failed to understand one assignment and received a poor mark. Stuart formed the view that, because of his poor mark, he would never become a carpenter. In his mind, he either had to do well on all his assignments or he was going to be a complete failure… as was predicted on many occasions by his former abusive partner.	Stuart should have considered his poor mark in the context of his overall performance. In reality, one poor mark is unlikely to affect his overall achievement. In any case, Stuart was able to identify why he had obtained the poor mark in that he misunderstood the goal of the assignment. In no way was this one poor mark consistent with his former partner's nasty predictions about his failure in the future. Indeed, when given his next assignment, all Stuart has to do is carefully consider what is being asked of him in the assignment and ask for clarification if needed if he wishes to avoid making the same mistake again.

Overgeneralisation	
After the end of his abusive relationship, Mark had met a nice person, Sophie, and a relationship was starting to develop. Sophie became stressed because of some things that happened at work and was more irritable than usual. Sophie snapped at Mark because of a minor thing he did that annoyed her in her irritated state. Mark became upset and Sophie became frustrated so a minor argument developed. Mark formed the view that his relationship with Sophie would not work because they had failed to communicate well on this one occasion. He believed that this argument could only lead to the same type of toxic and abusive relationship as the one he had previously endured. Mark ended the relationship with Sophie, seeing no point in trying to work things out.	Mark would have been better off to consider the one minor incident in the context of his other experiences with Sophie. Rather than this one argument reflecting an overall pattern of dysfunction in the relationship and a replay of the past abusive relationship, Mark could have formed the view that this demonstrated nothing more than the fact that people become more irritable if they have had a bad day. Mark could have understood that expressing irritability is not evidence of the type of abuse he had previously suffered.
Jumping to conclusions	
In his previous relationship, Ben had been on the receiving end of abuse on occasions when he made a mistake, had forgotten to do something or had failed to do it to his former partner's satisfaction. The abuse at these times was severe, and now, making mistakes tended to make Ben feel anxious. Ben made a small error at work, and even though his boss was unconcerned and brushed it off, Ben was sure that his boss really thought he was a hopeless individual who could not do his job properly. Ben began to worry that he was going to lose his job. He thought that his boss was just waiting for a chance to get rid of him.	Rather than jumping to the worst-case scenario, Ben would have felt better if he had been able to focus on the objective facts. Although he was concerned about the error he made, his boss did not agree. In rejecting what his boss told him, he failed to take into account that, logically, his boss had no reason to dismiss any criticisms of Ben's performance if the boss had any genuine concern. It was Ben's anxiety about making mistakes that created his worry, not any objective sign that his boss was dissatisfied.

Catastrophising	
Dylan had ignored his parents' repeated requests for him to leave his abusive partner. He had rejected the support his sister had offered him. Although he eventually left the relationship, he had not been ready to do so when his family had encouraged him to leave. Dylan had not been in touch with his family since his relationship with his abusive partner ended. He thought his parents and his sister would never forgive him for refusing their advice. He believed they would never speak to him again. Despite him finally having done what his family had wanted him to do and despite knowing they were loving people, Dylan believed that their rejection of him was inevitable.	Dylan formed a view about what would happen as a consequence of his disregard for the advice given by his parents and his sister. This view was inconsistent with what he knew about his family members. Given that he knew his parents and sister to be loving and caring people, the chances that they would reject Dylan were slim. Dylan was reacting to his own emotional response to his failure to listen to his parents rather than predicting a likely future. In any case, Dylan would not know how his parents and sister would respond to the news that he had left the abusive relationship until he spoke with them about the matter. Predicting a terrible future does not increase the chances that a terrible future will happen, especially if the prediction is based only on fears and not on other information, such as the loving nature of his family members, that Dylan knows to be true.

Personalisation	
John's best friend, who had stuck by him throughout his difficult and abusive relationship, had not been in touch for a couple of weeks. John was aware that his friend's mother had been very ill and was in hospital. John worried that his friend had abandoned him because John had recently disclosed to his friend the seriousness of the abuse he had experienced.	In reality, it seems that John's friend had a lot on his plate to deal with. It is unlikely, then, that his failure to be in touch was due to John disclosing the seriousness of the abuse he experienced. Sometimes, the simplest explanation is the best one. In all likelihood, John's friend was busy caring for his mother and his failure to be in touch had nothing to do with John.

Control fallacies	
Ian had had two major relationships in his life. The first began when he was quite young and lasted for several years. The relationship was unstable as they both grew into adulthood. The second relationship was the abusive one that was very difficult for Ian and caused him much distress. Ian formed the view that he was unlucky in relationships and there was nothing he could do about this. He felt he was doomed to repeat bad experiences in the future, no matter with whom he formed a relationship. As a result, Ian thought he should avoid relationships in the future.	Ian has fallen into the trap of believing that two unhappy experiences indicated control by some force he labelled as 'poor luck'. He could realise that both relationships had failed for very different reasons. He could also realise that the choices he makes about relationships in the future are his own and that the wisdom he has gained from bad experiences will help him avoid similar experiences in the future. Thinking in this better way, Ian could understand that it is not necessary to face a future alone.
Fallacy of fairness	
The more Brian thought about it, the more he thought it was unfair that he had had to endure the abuse he experienced in his relationship. He told himself that others did not have to put up with that sort of treatment, and it was not fair that he had to do so. He thought about what he had done for his partner and the way he had treated her well. He thought it was not fair that he had been on the receiving end of the abuse, given that he would never have behaved like that to her. Brian was driving himself crazy thinking about all the ways the world had been unfair to him. He found himself overwhelmed by feelings of anger and resentment.	It is a fact that, despite our best efforts, things do not always work out the way we want. Bad things can happen to anyone. Brian would be better off thinking that the world is neither fair nor unfair. Individuals are in charge of how they choose to conduct themselves. It was disappointing that Brian's ex-partner chose to behave aggressively and that she chose not to seek help for her anger management problems. However, her decisions did not indicate an unfair world.

Blaming	
Michael has been struggling since the end of his abusive relationship. He has been wondering whether it was the right thing to do to leave the relationship. In the few weeks since he left, he has found it difficult to establish a life for himself. Michael has been blaming himself for the problems in the relationship despite being the target of his ex-partner's abusive behaviour. He has been going over in his mind times when he now thinks he should have tried harder to please his partner or not done things that seemed to aggravate her. He keeps thinking that he is the one to blame for the difficulties he experienced.	It seems that Michael is blaming himself for his partner's abuse of him and the need to end the relationship primarily because he is struggling to cope in the aftermath of the end of the relationship. It would be better for Michael to understand his current difficulties as a result of the unwarranted abuse he endured. He had little choice but to leave the relationship if his long-term well-being was important to him. Certainly, his reasons for leaving were legitimate. Blaming himself because he is currently unhappy does not alter the fact that abuse of a partner is unwarranted and an act of violence, no matter its form. He was justified in leaving for that reason and because to stay would only have meant that he would have experienced more abuse.
Shoulds	
Craig thought he should have been doing better than he is currently. He recently left an abusive relationship, and he expected that things would have immediately improved. He thought that he should have looked for work by now and he should be socialising more with friends now that he is single. Craig is confused by his current situation. He is feeling intensely anxious much of the time but still believes he should be doing better and doing more than he is doing. He is disregarding the psychological impact of his relationship experiences.	Often, the demands we place on ourselves increase the pressure we feel. In reality, rather than demanding of himself that he do better, Craig would be better off choosing to do what is necessary for him to manage his anxiety and feel more settled before trying to achieve more challenging goals he might set for himself. Despite the demands we place on ourselves with thoughts like "I should…" and "I must…", much of what we choose to do or not do reflects preferences on our part rather than actual demands. Craig would be better off choosing to look after his mental health as a priority.

Emotional reasoning	
After the abusive relationship he endured, Nicholas reached the conclusion that he would never be in a relationship again because he was unlovable. He felt he had no redeeming qualities that would attract a partner. He believed he was going to be alone forever. The abuse Nicholas had experienced altered the way he thought about himself. Although previously secure, self-sufficient and well-adjusted, Nicholas understood he had changed because of the abuse. He now felt diminished by his experiences, unworthy and valueless.	Nicholas' strong emotional reaction to the abuse has caused him to believe that his views about his future are the 'truth'. Despite having no evidence that he will never find someone who would love him, he strongly believes this to be true only because he is feeling bad about himself. He has got this the wrong way around. At the moment, he is saying to himself, "Because I feel bad, the thing I fear is true". He would be better off exploring relationship opportunities when he is ready and then determining whether all this worry is necessary.
Fallacy of change	
Damien has a friend who experienced abuse in a relationship that was similar to the abuse Damien had experienced. Damien thought he had found someone who could truly understand what he had been going through. However, Damien's friend was never very comfortable talking about his feelings. In contrast, Damien was more able to talk about his emotional reactions to what had happened to him. Damien kept contacting his friend to talk about their similar experiences. Damien thought that his friend needed to open up and talk more about how he was feeling. He was disappointed and upset when his friend kept rejecting his efforts to meet up for a discussion.	Damien has made the mistake of assuming that because he values something, everyone else should value it, too. Damien is expecting his friend to change to meet his needs. Damien is upset because he believes his friend is deliberately withholding something from him that he strongly wants. He fails to see that he is upsetting himself by expecting his friend to change and offer Damien something his friend cannot provide. Damien would feel less stressed by this if he could accept that people cannot be expected to change to meet his needs and then look for support elsewhere.

Global labelling	
Brad is convinced he is hopeless and that he will fail at everything he tries to undertake. Brad formed this view as a result of the abusive relationship he experienced. His abusive girlfriend had repeatedly made comments about his worthlessness. She blamed him for her abusive behaviour, claiming Brad had failed to be the sort of person she was looking for. Brad formed the view that he just was not good enough and could not do anything right. He believed he would repeatedly fail so there was no point trying.	Brad's upset emotional state is colouring the way he views himself in a global sense. One relationship did not work out, and his abusive partner blamed him, so Brad decided that everything about him was terrible and he would fail at everything he undertook. The leap from the comments made by an abusive partner to a belief that he would never be able to do otherwise was illogical. He would have been better off seeing that one abusive person's views had no bearing on his successes in a future that did not even involve her.
Always being right	
Isaac realised he was a changed person because of his ex-partner's abusive behaviour towards him. His former partner was the sort of person who refused to let go of anything and always insisted she was right and, therefore, Isaac was wrong. Intense arguments would develop over minor matters because of her insistence on winning every argument. If he had tried to escape from these interactions, his ex-partner would follow him, demanding that he acknowledge she was right. Isaac had been exhausted by these interactions. However, she had been so insistent that she was right that Isaac has questioned his own point of view.	Isaac's ex-partner had caused problems by her insistence that the only acceptable outcome of an argument was for her to be 'proven' right. She refused to accept or understand that other people might hold an opinion different to her own. She was unable to feel ok herself if others disagreed with her. She could not understand that she could be fine if others saw things from a different perspective. She used her force of will to bring Isaac into line. This made Isaac confused and unhappy. Now, Isaac needed to learn to see his ex-partner's behaviour in the context of the errors she was making in her thinking.

Heaven's reward fallacy	
Despite the abuse he experienced from his former partner, prior to their break-up, Oscar had always put his partner's needs before his own. He ran around after her, listened to her problems and tried to help; he did all the housework and got her out of financial difficulties she had caused on numerous occasions. However, when he developed a problem of his own, Oscar was surprised that his ex-partner had been unwilling to do anything to help him. Despite all the effort he put into helping her, she refused to reciprocate. His ex-partner's failure to help him when he really needed assistance had hurt and confused Oscar. He thought he had done enough to earn some support from her.	Oscar had made the mistake of believing that because he had done the right thing his partner would do the same. Everyone is driven by their own motivations. Each person sets a standard for their own behaviour. Although it would be nice if others reciprocated, there is no guarantee that will happen when you enter into a relationship of any sort with another person.

It is apparent that these types of logical errors do not make things easy for us. Quite the opposite. They lead us to misinterpret events so that we adopt a limited or negative perspective that colours how we view things, our emotional responses, and the choices of how we behave as a consequence.

Why do we think in unhelpful ways?

Why do we think in ways that are distorted and not particularly helpful? To understand why errors in thinking happen, we have to consider the theory behind cognitive behaviour therapy (CBT). According to this theory, our thinking has more than one level. This is displayed in the diagram below.

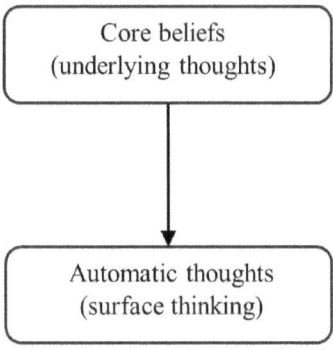

Figure 5: A diagram of the two levels of thought.

Automatic thoughts refer to the running commentary that goes through our heads as we go about our daily lives. If you pay attention, you will notice the constant chatter that goes on in your head about the things you are doing and how you are reacting to the people and events around you.

There is an easy exercise that will show you how this running commentary works. For the next minute, think about a bowl of fruit. Over the course of the minute, just let your thoughts do what they want as you think about a bowl of fruit. At the end of the minute, notice where your thoughts have taken you. Now consider the links between your starting point (thinking about a bowl of fruit) and where you ended up (thinking whatever it was you were thinking).

Consider below how this might have played out for one individual. This person started thinking about a bowl of fruit and ended up thinking about the need to become more financially secure. Follow their automatic thoughts.

> *Ok. I'm thinking about a bowl of fruit. I can picture a bowl of fruit. It's got bananas in it. I like bananas. I should buy some next time I go to the supermarket. I also need to get a loaf of bread. I must start a shopping list. Pay attention and think about a bowl of fruit. Oh, and milk, I mustn't forget milk. I hate running out of milk. Someone said once that they have orange juice on their cereal instead of milk. Yuck. I couldn't imagine anything worse. Not that I eat much cereal. I should eat more cereal... it's probably good for you. I will put cereal on my shopping list. But that might be a waste because I probably won't eat it. I have bought lots of things I thought would be good for me, but I never ate them. That reminds me that I should clean out the pantry. But I can't really find the time to do that at the moment. I am better of writing job applications so that I can get a better job and be more financially secure. I have to do something to be more financially secure.*

In contrast to automatic, surface thoughts, core beliefs refer to the underlying beliefs we have about how the world works and how we fit into that world. Core beliefs have an influence on our automatic thoughts. That is, we think the things we do on the surface because of our underlying beliefs about how things work. Unlike automatic thoughts, the content of our core beliefs is not readily available to us but can be examined by considering the content of our automatic thoughts.

So, where do the logical errors in thinking we have been talking about fit into this conceptualisation? Let's consider that in the diagram below.

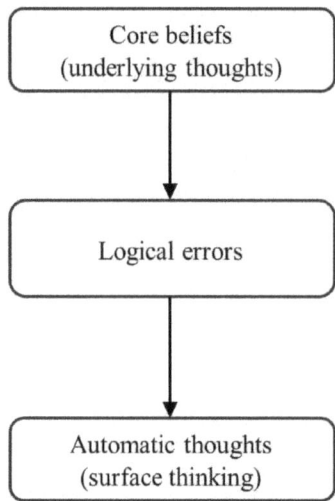

Figure 6: Where errors in thinking occur in our levels of thought.

The errors in thinking we make are a result of the core beliefs we hold. For example, if our core beliefs about the world and the future are that the world is threatening and the outlook is grim and pessimistic, then we are likely to inflate the degree of dangerousness we perceive and we are likely to catastrophise.

These logical errors then affect our surface thinking. We are more likely to be self-critical, tell ourselves everything is hopeless or tell ourselves that nothing is fair because of the logical errors we make based on our particular core beliefs. Logical errors are inevitable if there are problems with our core beliefs.

Our core beliefs are built on the basis of a variety of influences. These include our genetic makeup (e.g., an inherited overly reactive nervous system), our experiences (the things that happen to us), the messages we receive (the things people have said to us or the way they have treated us), and the ways we have interpreted these events. If the influences are positive and healthy, our core beliefs tend to be clear and logical errors are few. If the influences on us are negative, unhealthy or confusing, our core beliefs tend to be inaccurate, and the logical errors we make are many, and they strongly influence our automatic thoughts.

Underlying assumptions of logical errors

It has been suggested that each logical error is driven by specific assumptions. If our automatic thoughts are biased, then the biases are driven by our core beliefs and assumptions. Below are some examples of cognitive errors and examples of associated assumptions. Here we are referring to the assumptions that are inevitably made if the errors in our thinking are present.

Table 9: The assumptions underlying each logical error.

Cognitive error	Assumption
Filtering	The only events that matter are failures. I should measure myself by my errors.
Polarised thinking	Everything is always one extreme or the other.
Overgeneralisation	If it's true in one case, it must be true in every case that is even slightly similar.
Jumping to conclusions	If it has always been true in the past, it is going to be true in the future.
Catastrophising	Always think the worst because it is most likely to happen to you.
Personalisation	I am responsible for all bad things, failures, etc.
Control fallacies	You should be able to know in advance what is going to happen. You should have seen the bad thing coming before it happened.
Fallacy of fairness	The world is a fair place, and fairness influences how things turn out.
Blaming	Whether it is me or someone else, someone is always responsible when things are not the way I want them to be.
Shoulds	People have an obligation to do specific things that cannot be avoided.
Emotional reasoning	If a person feels bad, something must be wrong.
Fallacy of change	People must change to meet other people's needs.
Global labelling	A whole person and their entire life can be summed up by a single word (e.g., stupid).
Always being right	People have to choose a side, and there is a right side and a wrong side.

| Heaven's reward fallacy | Choosing to do good things for others will oblige others to do good things in return. |

Let's consider how these logical errors and the assumptions that are made affect automatic thoughts. Consider in this example what this person is saying to themselves about their relationship breakdown.

> *My head is spinning. I can't believe the relationship is over. It was a terrible time. I don't even know what went wrong, but I must have done something… or not done something to cause this to happen* (personalisation). *I am always so hopeless, and I'm never good enough* (global labelling). *It serves me right. I deserve to be in this mess* (blaming). *I should have seen it coming from the moment I met her and got out of there before things got this bad* (control fallacy).

Let's break this down and see where this person is making mistakes.

> Despite having been on the receiving end of the abuse in the relationship, he has assumed that he is the one responsible – that there was something he could have done differently to achieve a better outcome (personalisation). It seems unreasonable for him to hold this view.

> As a result of his version of his contribution to the relationship failing, he is self-critical and attributes certain characteristics to himself that attack him, not just in terms of the relationship problem, but in all things (global labelling). Even if he did make mistakes in his relationship, it does not follow that he is a bad or hopeless person deserving of bad things happening to him.

> Then, even though it was his partner who abused him in the relationship, he holds himself responsible and thinks he deserves what he has experienced (blaming). He is pointing the finger at himself despite having no evidence that he is the one who should be held accountable.

> Finally, even though he could not have controlled what happened, he believes he should have known in advance what was to come and then acted even before the abuse began (control fallacy). This suggests that he should have magically known in advance what was going to happen and he could have and should have controlled the end result.

The errors in this person's thinking have resulted in him feeling much worse than he would have if he had not made these errors. Let's find out how to change this way of thinking to protect yourself from the negative effects of logical errors.

Understanding automatic thoughts

The goal here is to teach you to think in a more realistic and balanced way so that you can cope better in the aftermath of the end of an abusive relationship. This is done in a number of steps. Let's begin this process.

Everybody experiences automatic thoughts. They reflect our way of making sense of and reacting to the world around us and to internal experiences, such as anxiety or memories and urges. Automatic thoughts are often highly believable, even when they are based on logical errors. As a result of their believability, we tend not to challenge them. If they pass unchallenged, they can have a profound and detrimental effect on our emotional state. For example, if a person thinks they are stupid and they do not challenge that thought, they are likely to feel upset and unworthy.

Consider this example.

> *"This must have been my fault. If only I could have been a better partner, maybe none of this would have happened. She kept telling me I didn't do the right thing... that I couldn't do anything right. Maybe if I had tried harder, things would have been better."*

It would be hard to think this way without feeling bad as a consequence. We tend to believe the things we tell ourselves. Even when we do not pay much attention to our self-talk – our running commentary – we can still be affected by it.

Catching automatic thoughts

It is important to pay attention to your automatic thoughts so that their content can be used to identify both the logical errors you are making and, ultimately, your core beliefs. The way to go about this is to keep a thought record related to times when you notice a change in the way you are feeling.

In its simplest form, a thought record asks you to identify the event that has occurred, to take notice of the thoughts that go through your head at the time of the event, and to record the consequences you experience, both in terms of how you feel and how you might act in response. Consider the example below of a simple thought record.

A	B	C
Activating event	Belief or thought	Consequence: emotional and behavioural
Adriana rang me and told me it was my fault that she had to leave me, and now the kids won't have their father.	*I should have tried harder and tolerated the abuse.*	*I felt really upset. I talked to a friend about whether I should forget about the abuse and beg her forgiveness.*

We do not usually pay much attention to the thoughts that go through our heads, even though they can have such a profound effect on how we are feeling and what we choose to do as a result of feeling that way. To change our thinking, we have to learn to identify our automatic thoughts. When we consider the events that trigger a response in us, we can usually identify what went through our mind at the time.

By keeping track of your automatic thoughts, you can learn patterns in your thinking that are linked with particular negative feelings and the behaviours you choose because you are feeling that way. Use the simple thought record below to keep track of your automatic thoughts in relation to events that stress you.

Simple automatic thoughts worksheet		
A	B	C
Activating event	Belief or thought	Consequence: emotional and behavioural

Worksheet available at elemen.com.au

Understanding and noticing logical errors

Everyone makes logical errors. It is important to understand this point. It is when the error you are making (e.g., everything should be fair) conflicts with how things really are (e.g., the world is neither fair nor unfair; it just is the way it is) that problems arise. However, it is also important to be able to recognise the logical errors you are making so that you can correct them and correct the problems in your core beliefs. To do this, you can try the simple approach of expanding on your thought record form so that you include the types of logical errors that are reflected in your automatic thoughts.

Let's go back to our original thought record form and expand the examples.

Expanded thought record form- example			
A	B	C	D
Activating event	Belief or thought	Consequence: emotional and behavioural	Logical errors
Adriana rang me and told me it was my fault that she had to leave me, and now the kids won't have their father.	*I should have tried harder and tolerated the abuse.*	*I felt really upset. I talked to a friend about whether I should forget about the abuse and beg her forgiveness.*	*Blaming (self)*

This person accepted Adriana's statement and blamed himself for Adriana's decision to leave and the abuse he experienced. He held himself responsible for things that were not in his control.

Below is an expanded thought record form that you can use to identify your logical errors in what you are thinking.

Expanded thought record form			
A	B	C	D
Activating event	Belief or thought	Consequence: emotional and behavioural	Logical errors

Worksheet available at elemen.com.au

Reframing your thoughts (cognitive restructuring)

The process of challenging our negative automatic thoughts is called cognitive restructuring. This is what we are trying to achieve here. The conclusions we reach because of our logical errors can be challenged and replaced with something that is healthier and more accurately reflects how the world really works.

Although there are lots of ways you can go about restructuring your thinking, we are going to introduce you to a straightforward method. We are going to start by ensuring that you understand the difference between fact and opinion. This is important as our thoughts and decision-making should be based on facts and not the opinions we form because of incorrect information that can underlie our core beliefs. For example, an opinion would be "I am stupid". You might form this opinion because someone has repeatedly told you that you are stupid or because they acted in a way that encouraged you to believe you were stupid. It is not the truth or a fact that you are stupid. It is a belief you have or an opinion you have formed because of incorrect information.

We refer to the opinion on which you rely as a work of fiction. That is, you write a story in your head about what is happening and then act as if the story is true. You need to be able to identify when you are relying on the story you have written in your mind rather than basing your thoughts on factual evidence. Let's start by having a go at identifying fact from opinion or fiction. In the spaces provided, you can add other things you have been thinking and consider whether they are facts or opinions.

Fact or fiction worksheet		
Statement	*Fact*	*Fiction*
I am stupid		√
I love bushwalking	√	
I am ugly		
I forgot to renew my driver's licence		
No one likes me		
This will be a disaster		
I'm not good enough		
I am single		

I will never fall in love again		
I hate my job		
I should have known what was about to happen		
There are times when people feel stressed		

Checklist available at elemen.com.au

The facts here are:

    I love bushwalking

    I forgot to renew my driver's licence

    I am single

    I hate my job

    There are times when people feel stressed

The statements that are opinions are:

    I am stupid

    I am ugly

    No one likes me

    This will be a disaster

    I'm not good enough

    I will never fall in love again

    I should have known what was about to happen

Why should we make this distinction between what is a fact and what is an opinion? It is because the errors in thinking we make are based on opinion and not on fact. Further, because we hold this opinion, we assume that it is true because we are thinking it and not because it is based on fact.

To tidy up our thinking and remove the logical errors, we have to rely on those thoughts that are based on fact alone. We can reject thoughts that are just based on our opinions unless they align with fact because our opinions can be faulty. Factual information will be a good guide for us to determine whether or not we should believe what we are thinking. Consider the following example.

Cognitive restructuring worksheet - Example
What I am thinking *I am thinking that I should have tried harder and behaved differently so that Adriana would not have been forced to treat me so badly.*
Facts supporting the thought *She might have said I should have tried harder but that is not a fact.*
Facts contradicting the thought *I did all I could to cope with the abuse.* *I was abused whether or not I had done anything wrong.* *Throughout our relationship, Adriana often blamed me for her wrongdoing.* *Adriana had abused other partners in the past.* *Adriana was not forced to treat me and her other partners in an abusive manner.*
Is this thought based on factual evidence or opinion? *It seems that my thoughts are just based on an opinion. It was an opinion that Adriana expressed and then I believed her and adopted her opinion. No one is responsible for Adriana's behaviour and decisions except for Adriana.*

By looking at the facts for and against a point of view being true, you can work out the value of holding that opinion. It seems like a waste of time to be thinking a particular thing and being negatively affected by it emotionally and behaviourally if you cannot even determine that the opinion reflects the truth. You can use the worksheet below to examine your thoughts in terms of the facts supporting what you are thinking and the facts that contradict what you are thinking.

Cognitive restructuring worksheet
What I am thinking
Facts supporting the thought
Facts contradicting the thought
Is this thought based on factual evidence or opinion?

Worksheet available at elemen.com.au

Rather than looking at facts for and against the truth of your thoughts, another very easy approach to reframing your thinking is what is called compassionate cognitive restructuring. Here, you are asked to look at your thoughts in a more compassionate way. Ask yourself what you would say to a person who is in a similar situation to you. In all likelihood, you would say something much kinder and closer to the truth than you are saying to yourself.

Consider this example.

Example:	
Your friend says:	*She only hit me because I wasn't a good enough partner. She only left because I wasn't good enough.*
You might say:	*That's not true. I know you did all you could to make that relationship work. But the truth is, she is an aggressive person who hits her partner when things aren't going her way. Her decisions to do these things are hers. There was nothing you could have done to make it stop. If there was, you would have done it.*

It is the case that we often are harder on ourselves than others think is necessary. We set higher standards. For example, you might say that you should never make a mistake and call yourself stupid if you do. Your friend would say that everyone makes mistakes and all we can do is learn from them.

It is interesting that, although you trust your good friends, you choose not to believe them when they make an honest, positive statement about you. Remember how it feels when the reverse occurs when you make a positive statement to your friend, and they dismiss what you say or reject it in favour of a statement you see as false. It is frustrating. You can be as kind and supportive to yourself as you are to the people you care about.

Making the restructured thinking habitual

To get to a point where you are thinking in a healthier way, you need to go through a process of deliberately challenging your thinking. You need to overlearn to notice your automatic thoughts and then reframe them into healthier and more accurate alternative thoughts. You will then move on to challenging your thinking and adjusting your automatic thoughts without giving it as much attention. Eventually, you will not even have to do that because your core beliefs will be corrected to offer you a more accurate template of how the world works and how you fit into that world.

Targeting the assumptions

Let's not forget about those assumptions that underlie the errors you make in your thinking. You need to challenge those assumptions to completely correct your thinking. Remember, if the assumption that underlies the error is shown to be wrong, there is every reason to abandon the logical error and replace it with a more logical point of view.

There are a few ways you can challenge the assumptions that underlie logical errors. We are going to focus on three approaches. Firstly, we are going to apply the strategy of looking at the advantages and disadvantages of holding an assumption. Consider the following example of someone who is predicting that things are going to work out poorly.

Assumption worksheet: Advantages and disadvantages
Logical error and assumption *Catastrophising. Always think the worse because it is most likely going to happen to you.*
Advantages *I will always be on 'red alert' in case something happens.*
Disadvantages *I will be on 'red alert' all the time, even when it is not necessary for me to be so.* *I will find it hard to feel any joy about anything if I constantly worry about everything going wrong.* *I will waste a lot of time worrying about things that end up not being as bad as I thought they were going to be.*

Challenging the assumption that underlies a tendency to catastrophise, you can see that there are many more disadvantages to doing this than there are advantages. In fact, experiencing the disadvantages may turn out to be worse than the possible thing in the future you are worrying about.

Secondly, you can act against the assumptions. What would happen if the assumption was incorrect? Consider the following example.

Assumption worksheet: Acting against the assumption
Logical error and assumption *Catastrophising. Always think the worst because it is most likely going to happen to you.*
Things that might happen if I acted like the assumption was not true *I might be able to relax and feel calmer.* *I might find some enjoyment in the things I do.* *I might experience some peace of mind.* *I might look forward to some things in the future.*

By acting as if the assumption is false, you can usually identify the positive things that would occur as a consequence. All of these things are better than predicting a gloomy future. Remember, spending your time thinking about how badly things are likely to turn out in the future also removes all the pleasure from the present.

Finally, you can argue against the assumption. You can take the perspective that the assumption is wrong and develop an argument for your case. Consider the following example.

Assumption worksheet: Arguing against the assumption
Logical error and assumption *Catastrophising. Always think the worse because it is most likely to happen to you.*
Arguments against the assumption *Thinking something might happen will not make it happen.* *There is no cosmic force that is directing all bad things my way.*

Here, you are thinking of the *facts* that can be used to present a good argument that the assumption associated with the logical error is not accurate. This will allow you to challenge your error-ridden thinking and replace it with healthier thinking that will not encourage you to feel strong, negative emotions.

Below is a worksheet you can use to challenge the assumptions that underlie your errors in thinking.

Targeting assumptions worksheet
Logical error and assumption
Advantages
Disadvantages
Things that might happen if I acted like the assumption was not true
Arguments against the assumption

Worksheet available at elemen.com.au

Here, we have asked you to consider challenging the sorts of thoughts you might have that are likely to make you feel worse than you would otherwise feel if you did not think that way. You have learned to access these logical errors by paying attention to your automatic thoughts that serve as the running commentary your mind provides. You have learned ways to challenge these errors and remove them and their influence from your thinking. The goal of doing these things has been to help you manage your distress and protect yourself from distress in the future. It then becomes important to re-establish some things you have lost as a result of being in an abusive relationship. We will consider these next.

Re-establish a sense of self and self-worth

Your sense of self refers to your perception of who you are, your traits and characteristics that define you. Your sense of self allows you to know who you are and guides you in terms of what you stand for. People with a strong sense of self understand their own value even if they sometimes make mistakes or sometimes make poor decisions.

Self-worth refers to the belief you have in your value as a person. People with high self-worth understand they are deserving of respect, love and consideration just because of who they are rather than because of what they have earned.

Factors that enhance a sense of self and self-worth

There are a variety of factors that are associated with your sense of self and your feelings of self-worth. They are the things that can define your sense of self and your understanding of who you are. They are also the things that can be damaged by the experiences you have during a relationship with an abusive partner.

Your personal values

Your values relate to how you understand right from wrong. They are associated with what you choose to stand for. Living up to the standards you set can enhance your sense of self and your self-worth.

Your self-assurance

Self-assurance is associated with a calm sense of acceptance of yourself and a belief in yourself. It implies a certainty of who you are without reliance on other's perceptions of you or trying to copy other people's identity.

Your interests

Seeking out hobbies and activities that reflect your interests can enhance your self-worth. This is because you are doing things that give you pleasure, provide you with opportunities for achievement and satisfaction, and give you a defined sense of who you are and what you enjoy.

Your emotional stability

The more emotionally stable you feel, the better your self-worth. This is particularly the case if you learn to respond appropriately to self-criticism, rejecting the damaging effects of excessive self-criticism in favour of self-care.

The fulfilment you get from relationships

Here, we are not talking about what others might want in their relationships but what would be fulfilling for you. One factor that will enhance your self-worth is a belief in your worthiness to be loved and to offer love.

Employment

Although career pathways can be stressful and put too much pressure on you, being gainfully employed can be associated with your self-worth. The sense of satisfaction you can gain from being financially self-sufficient, and your ability to look after yourself can boost your sense of self and your self-worth.

These features can be fundamental to your sense of self-worth and offer opportunities for you to improve your sense of self and develop your feelings of self-worth. Additionally, there are other ways that you can enhance your self-worth.

How to build self-worth

Develop a support network

A support system of family and friends can act as a buffer against the stress you experience at challenging times in your life. Turning to others for support when you need help is a useful thing to do. The people you turn to can help you build your self-worth by helping you realise how valued you are by these people.

Avoid comparing yourself to others

Do not try to determine where you should be in life by making comparisons between yourself and others. Everyone follows their own path through life, experiencing different things along the way. It is not useful to make unrealistic comparisons that only serve to undermine your self-worth, even though these comparisons are based on unreasonable standards you have set for yourself.

Be compassionate with yourself

Unconstructive self-criticism never really helps anyone. Instead, use a strengths-based approach to life by building on what you do well rather than focusing on what you struggle to do well, that is, a deficits-based approach. Be kind to yourself and recognise that you can choose to do more of what you do best rather than criticise yourself for failing to do the things you cannot do.

Consider your role in the lives of other people

Give some thought to the meaning you have for the people in your life that you care about and who are about you. It is not really for you to judge how much you mean to them. It is up to them to decide this. Even if you do not see yourself as worthy, recognise that others may see you as an essential and much-loved person in their lives.

Be inspired by others in a similar situation to you

Try to be like those people you respect. Learn from their experiences. Gain wisdom from what they have been through and successfully managed.

Find a challenge

Take a step outside your comfort zone and undertake a challenge that stretches you. Do something you have not done before. Congratulate yourself on your achievements.

Understand it is not what happens…

The importance here is to develop an understanding that it is not what happens to you that will determine your self-worth but how you respond to what happens to you. That is, experiencing difficult things in life will not determine who you are as a person. You just need to remember that you are responsible for and in control of how you think about a situation and what you choose to do.

You can select your preferred ways of enhancing your self-worth or use all of these suggestions. Certainly, there is no one individual thing that will be effective. Rather, it is an accumulation of factors that impact on how you view yourself and your worth.

In addition to the things you can do to improve your self-worth, consideration should be given to how you think and the beliefs you hold and their impact on your self-worth. Before moving on, let's consider ways you can think that will have an impact on your view of yourself.

Thoughts and beliefs to promote high self-worth

We know that the way we think can affect how we feel and what we choose to do. Let's consider the types of thoughts that can improve self-worth.

> *"I am worthy of love no matter what I have or haven't done in the past."*
>
> Although you need to take responsibility for your actions, there is no need to denigrate yourself for what you have done. Learn from mistakes and move on.

"What I have does not define who I am."

It is not what or how much you have or own that will determine your self-worth. It is helpful to recognise that 'things' can be impermanent. Things change, accidents happen, and relationships come to an end.

"I have the right to feel whatever it is I am feeling."

To achieve self-worth, you do not have to be happy all the time. That is not what will establish your self-worth. As human beings, we are capable of a full range of emotions, and they all have a purpose. They allow us to express ourselves. It is reasonable to acknowledge and experience our emotions.

"There is no reason to be afraid of being alone."

People with high self-worth will make time for themselves and not fear being left out of things. They are not overly concerned about how other people view them. People invited into their lives will receive that invitation because they have earned the right.

Working on developing your sense of self and your self-worth are useful undertakings because of the effect that an abusive relationship can have on how you view yourself. However, there is another important aspect of how we function that may need to be re-established. Here, we are referring to self-efficacy.

Re-build your self-efficacy

Self-efficacy refers to your belief that you can do what you set out to do. The word 'efficacy' means 'the ability to produce a desired or intended result'. We are going to consider the ways in which the experience of abusive relationships can affect self-efficacy. We will also look at ways to restore self-efficacy.

The concept of self-efficacy

The idea of self-efficacy was initially developed by a Canadian-American psychologist named Albert Bandura. He identified self-efficacy as an important feature of how you think, how you feel, and how you motivate yourself. Self-efficacy contributes to:

> How much effort you put into a task
>
> How you will persist with a task
>
> How resilient you are in response to challenges that might prevent you from achieving your goal.

People with high self-efficacy are usually confident in how they approach a task. When faced with obstacles, they view them as able to be overcome. They also are ambitious in the goals they set. In contrast, people with low self-efficacy tend to doubt their ability to complete a task. They cope poorly with the challenges they might face. They are more likely to give up and not complete a task when they are confronted with a setback.

Interestingly, self-efficacy can vary across different areas in your life. For example, you may have high self-efficacy in relation to your work tasks but low self-efficacy with regard to relationships.

The link between self-efficacy and relationship abuse

There are a number of factors that influence your self-efficacy. Importantly, self-efficacy is affected by the experiences you have in life. In this way, relationship abuse can impact your level of self-efficacy. These types of experiences undermine your belief that you can do what you set out to do.

Why is self-efficacy important?

Self-efficacy is important because of the role it plays in how you feel about yourself and whether you are able to pursue and successfully achieve your life goals. With low self-efficacy, you may not even try to undertake a task or strive for a goal because you simply believe that you are not capable of achieving what you set out to do. This can significantly limit your life in many ways.

Ways to improve self-efficacy

Here, we have identified things you can do to build your self-efficacy. They are straightforward methods of building your confidence in your belief that you can do what you set out to do.

Set goals that are achievable

Do not set yourself up to fail by setting goals that are too hard to achieve. Instead, set goals that are manageable and achievable. You are better off striving for an easier goal with a greater certainty of success than aiming for a bigger goal that is unlikely to be achieved. The goals you set can be more difficult or challenging as you become more confident in your ability to do what you set out to do. Consider this example.

> *George had been having a tough time. He had lost his previous job a while back because of the problems he experienced as a result of the abusive relationship he was in. George wanted to get another job, but the thought of doing so was overwhelming. He wasn't sure he could do that and be of use to an employer. He decided to take things a step at a time. George thought it best to just focus on the things he had to do to get his life in order, such as dealing with the bank. He thought that when everything was going smoothly, he might undertake a training course and then when he was ready, re-enter the workforce. He felt more confident about doing it this way than jumping in the deep end. He was worried that if he tried to get a job immediately, he would fail.*

Break down tasks into smaller, achievable goals

A good approach to building your self-efficacy is to break down your goals into smaller, manageable tasks. By doing this, you are likely to feel less overwhelmed by the enormity of what you are trying to achieve. When you successfully achieve the smaller goals, your confidence in your capacity to do what you set out to do will be enhanced.

> *William had been staying with family since he left the abusive relationship. He knew he had to find a place to live but felt unable to even think about what he would have to do to move into a new home. William's sister helped him break down the task into smaller steps that William could undertake without feeling the task was impossible. They made a list for William to work on. On the list were tasks such as the two of them visiting various neighbourhoods to see which appealed to William, investigating whether William was entitled to rental assistance from the government, looking on the real estate rental website, and visiting properties with his sister that William was interested in viewing. Approaching each of the tasks separately, William felt more confident that he could find himself somewhere to live.*

Imagine succeeding

We often undermine our success in undertaking a task by predicting failure. Instead, you should picture yourself successfully completing the task and achieving your goal. When you are faced with a particular challenge, imagine what it would be like to go ahead and do what you set out to do.

> *On the advice of the police, Lawrence had to go to court to seek a restraining order against his abusive former partner, who had been threatening him since he left the relationship. He was dreading having to do so, imagining himself freezing in court and not being able to convey the problems he faced. On the advice of a friend, Lawrence decided to picture himself in his mind undertaking this task with confidence. He pictured what he would be wearing to improve his confidence, he pictured walking into the court with his lawyer and taking a seat. He imagined himself talking in court and relating what he had been experiencing. He pictured himself speaking clearly and coherently. He imagined what it would be like when he was granted the restraining order. He pictured himself walking out of the court with his head held high.*

Look for positive role models

Look for people who you know can successfully do what you want to be able to do. Examine the ways in which they go about the task and identify the strategies they use. If you feel comfortable, ask them how they succeed in the tasks they undertake.

> *Martin's confidence in his ability to follow through and do the things he needed to do had been undermined by his long-term, abusive relationship. He had been repeatedly told by his former partner that he was stupid and incapable of doing anything. However, now that Martin had left the relationship, he knew things had to change. He knew that he had to take charge of his life, no matter how lacking in confidence he felt. So, Martin decided to ask for advice from his friend, who had been through a similar relationship but had managed to move on and be successful in his life after the end of the relationship. This friend was happy to help Martin.*

Reflect on successes you have had in the past

Remember times in the past when you were faced with a challenge or undertook a task you no longer feel able to do now, but you have successfully done what you set out to do in the past. Reflect on times when you have been faced with difficult things and managed to deal with them. Everyone has been successful some of the time.

> *Since he experienced the abuse in his relationship with his former partner, Malcolm felt he couldn't cope with even the smallest of problems he faced in life. He had always believed himself to be a self-sufficient and competent person until he met his former partner when everything changed. Malcolm was convinced he could no longer function well enough to move on with his life. He felt hopeless and adrift. Malcolm's counsellor asked him to consider times he had coped with things in the past. Malcolm told the counsellor about the breakdown of his relationship with the mother of his daughter that occurred before he met his abusive partner. He recalled that it had been a difficult time, and he had been very sad but had done what he could to ensure his daughter felt secure and happy. He said he had established a home for them, got a job, arranged daycare for his daughter, and set himself up financially. He recalled feeling proud of his ability to ensure her daughter's well-being.*

Positive self-talk

Stop thinking in self-doubting and negative ways. Instead, engage in thinking that is encouraging and positive. This does not require you say over-the-top and unrealistically positive things to yourself. Positive and encouraging self-talk, for example, may be something like, "I will do the best that I can".

> *It was pointed out to Charles by his counsellor that he was engaging in the type of self-talk that was likely to undermine his confidence and self-efficacy. Paying attention to what he was saying to himself, Charles realised his counsellor was right. So, he tried to change his thinking. He was kinder to himself. He recognised that he was trying his hardest and that he could not expect more of himself. He praised himself for achieving his goals, even if they were small ones. Charles was able to see that this type of self-talk made him feel more settled and more confident.*

Accept failures and learn from them

Recognise that it is unlikely that you will succeed in all you undertake. This is a normal part of life. We learn from our mistakes. These types of experiences cause us to make different and better choices in the future.

> *Samuel was frustrated. He was trying hard to get his life back in order, but things didn't always work out the way he had expected. He didn't get the job he wanted and missed out on the rental property he most wanted. He started to feel quite despondent, blaming himself for these failures. He started to tell himself he was hopeless and couldn't do what he set out to achieve. But Samuel's friends told him he was being unnecessarily harsh. So, he stopped and thought about what he was doing and how he was undermining himself by being so critical. Samuel took a deep breath and realised that everyone makes mistakes and fails to achieve the things they want at some point in their lives. He gave some consideration to how he could do things differently so that he improved his chances of success. This required that he look at his 'failures' objectively rather than seeing them as evidence of his hopelessness.*

Seek feedback that is constructive

A lot of people will tell you what you should do. The flood of advice can be confusing and overwhelming. You need to remember that much of this advice is just the opinion of the advice giver and not 'the truth'. It is better to seek out constructive criticism from people you truly trust and who have a history of giving good advice.

> *Stefan was being pulled in lots of different directions. Everyone he spoke with about his situation had different advice for him. One person told him to take legal action to ensure his former partner was left with nothing. Another person told him he hadn't tried hard enough to make the relationship work. Every time he turned to someone, Stefan was given a different opinion about what he 'should do'. So, Stefan decided to take a step back from all of these confusing suggestions. He knew he needed to find ways to build his confidence to allow himself to move forward. Stefan made the decision to turn to the people who always had his best interests in mind, that is, his mother and father. He trusted them and knew they only wanted the best for him. He pushed away all the voices of others in his mind and listened only to the advice he received from his parents.*

Build a network of supportive people

Put together a support network of people who can offer you good support in your decision-making. These should be people who believe in you and who will boost your confidence in yourself. These people can be friends and family or, mentors and professionals, or a combination of all.

> *When Gavin's relationship with his abusive partner ended, he felt he was unable to cope and wouldn't be able to get his life on track. However, he also knew that he had to find a way to do what he needed to improve his life situation. He knew he needed help. So, he contacted a number of people to assist him with the things he knew he had to do. He sought out a financial counsellor at a welfare organisation to help him work out what he needed to do to be secure. He re-engaged with a person who had previously been a close and supportive friend, seeking and receiving moral support. He reached out to his family for comfort. He obtained a referral to a mental health counsellor and engaged in a therapeutic relationship with that person. As he thought of things he needed to do, he sought out people who could assist him in achieving his goals. He only selected people who would encourage him to take charge of his life rather than those who seemed to want to take over his life.*

Take small risks

It is all right to step outside your comfort zone and take small risks. Indeed, this is the way you will build your confidence by achieving the goals you set. Remember that you do not have to take enormous risks. Smaller ones will increase your chances of succeeding which is important in confidence building.

> *Since the end of his abusive relationship, David had been trying to keep everything manageable in his life. He felt less anxious when he acted in a cautious manner. He stayed at home and just focused on managing the day-to-day demands of running his home. But David realised that doing this wasn't helping him. His confidence wasn't improving, and he just didn't trust his ability to do more than he was already doing. He knew he couldn't go on like this. So, the first thing David did was accept an invitation from a friend to catch up for a coffee. David thought he would feel really exposed in public and wouldn't feel comfortable, but it turned out that he had a nice time. He then contacted an old friend and asked if he wanted to go fishing with him. David then looked online for a short training course that would interest him and selected one that would extend his computer skills, thinking this might help him when he was ready to apply for a job. As he started to do these things, David realised they were becoming easier to do. He could feel his confidence building.*

Practice resilience

Find ways to bounce back when you have had to deal with difficult times. In this way, you can develop resilience. Resilience refers to the ability to recover from or to withstand the challenges and difficulties you face in life.

> *Niall knew the relationship he had with his abusive former partner had changed him. Even after the relationship ended, he had felt downtrodden. People who knew him before had commented that he was not the same happy person he had been earlier in his life. Niall knew he had to make some decisions. He didn't want to be like this and feel like this for the rest of his life. He realised that any change had to come from inside himself. Niall made up his mind he was going to confront life fully. He was going to find ways to meet life demands with courage, knowing that having courage didn't mean doing things without fear but doing them despite the fear. He was determined to be optimistic that he could have a good life in the future. Niall decided that his best response to a person who had tried to subdue him and diminish him was to refuse to be subdued or diminished. He knew all of this might be difficult to achieve, but he was determined to do his best nonetheless.*

Following these suggestions, you can build your belief in your ability to do things that you want to do. Next, we need to examine ways you can stand up for yourself, a skill that might have been undermined by the abusive relationship you experienced.

Understand your rights

We are often not clear about our rights, particularly those that relate to our ability to take charge of our lives. Let's look at some of the mistaken assumptions we make that may be related to your current situation and then consider your legitimate rights. We will also consider how holding these mistaken assumptions might affect how you react following an abusive relationship and how abandoning the mistaken assumptions may improve your situation.

Table 10. Mistaken assumptions, their consequences and your legitimate rights.

Mistaken assumption	*It is selfish to put your needs before the needs of others.*
Consequence	You may end up not receiving the help and support you need to deal with the emotional costs of the abuse you experienced. This is because you may not ask for help and support for yourself if other people are suffering as well or if you think others are too busy with their own lives.
Legitimate right	You have a right to put yourself first some of the time.
Outcome	Understanding your right may allow you to ask for the help and support your need at this difficult time. The extent to which a person can offer you help and support should be determined by them and not by you.
Mistaken assumption	*You shouldn't take up other's valuable time with your own problems.*
Consequence	No one knows you need help if you do not say so. As a consequence, you do not receive the help you need.
Legitimate right	You have a right to ask for help or emotional support.
Outcome	The people who care about you will understand you need help, and they can offer you help if they are able.
Mistaken assumption	*People don't want to hear that you feel bad, so keep it to yourself.*
Consequence	Your feelings are never expressed, and you end up feeling bottled up and isolated.

Legitimate right	You have a right to feel and express pain.
Outcome	You will be able to feel some relief by sharing how you feel. Your emotional pain is not harmful to others who care about you. Friendships should be equal and reciprocal in that you should support your friends, and they should support you in times of distress. Accepting that people may be concerned about you frees you to express how you are feeling and allows your friends to do something for you at a time when it probably seems to them there is little they can do to make things better.
Mistaken assumption	*When someone takes the time to give you advice, you should take it seriously.*
Consequence	You may be overwhelmed by people who are telling you what you should do. Unfortunately, the advice from one person can conflict with the advice from another which only increases your confusion.
Legitimate right	You have a right to ignore the advice of others.
Outcome	You will come to realise that the advice people give you is only their opinion and the final decision will be yours to make. You should not then feel pressured to do what others demand or expect, especially if it contradicts with what you need.
Mistaken assumption	*You should always try to accommodate others. If you don't, they won't be there when you need them.*
Consequence	You will be so busy thinking about what others need that you will have no opportunity to consider your own needs.
Legitimate right	You have a right to say no.
Outcome	You are the only person who truly knows how you are feeling so you need to be the person who decides what you can take on and what you cannot. By understanding you have the right to say no, you can pay attention to your own needs when they are greater than the needs of others.

Mistaken assumption	*Don't be anti-social. People are going to think you don't like them if you say you'd rather be alone instead of with them.*
Consequence	You will have no opportunity to have time by yourself to reflect on what has happened and how you are feeling if you give in to the demands of others to do what they are offering, such as ensuring people are around you all the time.
Legitimate right	You have a right to be alone, even if others would prefer your company.
Outcome	By understanding you have a right to time to yourself, you may be able to strike a good balance between being around others and being alone to deal with your thoughts and feelings.
Mistaken assumption	*You should have a good reason for what you feel and do.*
Consequence	You waste energy thinking about how you are presenting yourself to others and worrying about what they think about you.
Legitimate right	You have a right not to have to justify yourself to others.
Outcome	Particularly at times of intense distress, you should be able to express yourself without having to explain yourself to others who may have chosen to do things differently if they were in your situation.
Mistaken assumption	*When someone is in trouble, you should help them.*
Consequence	This may cause you to ignore your own needs in favour of the needs of others. This can result in your needs never being met.
Legitimate right	You have a right not to take responsibility for someone else's problem.
Outcome	There are times in life when your needs exceed the needs of others, even if they are facing problems of their own. Understanding this may free you to focus on your own emotional reactions without worrying about the emotional reactions of others.

Mistaken assumption	*It is not nice to put people off. If questioned, give an answer.*
Consequence	Believing you must answer people's questions, you may feel pressured to discuss things you do not want to discuss at times when you are not feeling able to discuss them.
Legitimate right	You have a right to choose not to respond to a situation.
Outcome	Curiosity on the part of the questioner does not give them the right to know your private business or you an obligation to respond to their questioning. You are the person who decides what you disclose and when you disclose it. By accepting this, you can maintain your privacy if that is what you choose.

In many cases, asserting your legitimate rights is largely a matter of you accepting that these rights are legitimate and then calmly acting on that understanding. However, in other cases, you will be required to respond to a demand from someone else. Learning to be assertive can help you stand up for your rights.

Learn to be assertive

Another useful focus of our attention is on assertive communication. We need to consider your assertiveness skills because you are likely to be faced with many challenging interactions that occur after an abusive relationships end. These may include personal issues, such as negotiating matters related to the end of the relationship and more practical things, such as living arrangements, property settlements or, importantly, parenting arrangements if you have children. However, assertiveness skills may also be useful in a more general sense if your ability to assert yourself has been undermined by the abuse you experienced.

Assertiveness refers to standing up for your rights without trampling over the rights of others. Some people mistake assertiveness for aggressiveness which refers to the aggressive assertion of your rights irrespective of the rights of others. At the other extreme is passivity where a person will not stand up for their own rights and allow others to walk over them.

So, the aim here is to teach you to stand up for your own rights without disregarding the rights of other people. An assertive interpersonal style will allow you to negotiate for what you want without demanding that it happen.

Asking for change

Firstly, we need to consider how to assertively solve problems by making reasonable requests for change or appropriate requests for what we would like to have happen. Many people find this difficult. They will start to make a request but are easily derailed by the deflection techniques used by the other person. Alternatively, they will start to make a request but are then affected by the annoyance they feel about the response of the other person. The step-by-step guide below is designed to help you plan ahead for how you are going to manage a request for change.

Define the problem situation

You should start by defining the problem you are facing. Do this by focusing on the facts of the matter and not your interpretation of the situation. You should do this by being as specific as possible. Avoid generalisations like "It's always the case…" or "Nothing ever goes right…". So, keep a narrow focus on the situation you have identified that you wish to change. Limit this to one problem at a time rather than bombarding the other person with a list of grievances.

> *Despite my repeated requests for you to make arrangements for me or someone in my family to collect my belongings, this has not occurred.*

Describe how you are feeling

Here, you get a chance to describe how you feel about the situation. Remember, you are referring to how you feel and not how someone else *made* you feel. Be clear about the link between your feelings and the problem situation. Again, do not generalise to all situations or all problems.

Avoid blaming others. By blaming others, you put them on the defensive and little is ever resolved as a consequence. When you talk about how you are feeling, use what is called an 'I message'. That is, your descriptions of your feelings should start with something like "I feel…". No one can argue with you about this matter. They cannot say that you do not feel something that you have stated you feel. If you started with "You make me feel…", it is likely that the other person would argue that it was not their intention to make you feel that way, and if you do, that is your problem. Using 'I messages' allows you to avoid all of that type of discussion. In any case, you are the person who decides how you feel, and you should be able to relate that feeling to the other person.

This is a good opportunity to express your feelings. It is a mistake to assume that others know what you are thinking or feeling if you have not said so. If you have not said how you feel, the other person can do little more than guess. We make a mistake by assuming that someone who knows you well can 'mindread' and automatically know what you are thinking or feeling. Clear communication works much better than allowing others to guess.

> *I am disappointed that this arrangement hasn't been made and annoyed it has gone on for so long.*

Make your request for change

Here, you should make a statement about what you want to happen. You need to be brief. Do not turn your request into a lecture. Also, you need to be specific. Clearly state what you want rather than use terms that are not concrete. For example, it will not help to say, "I want you to leave me alone" because that is a generalised statement that can be interpreted in a multitude of ways. You would be better off saying, "I want you to stop contacting me by phone or on social media," or "I want you to stop driving past my house".

> *I want an arrangement made for me or one of my family members to collect my belongings this weekend, on either Saturday or Sunday.*

Outline possible positive consequences

If the other person initially does not want to agree with your request, you may choose to point out the positive consequences that would follow on from agreement. Do not make wild promises. Just focus on the positive things that are likely to happen from the change you are requesting. You are building the argument for what you want. For example, you could say, "I want you to remove my name from your lease. If you do this, I will agree to you keeping the furniture".

> *If I or a family member can collect my belongings this weekend, I will make no claims on household items that we jointly purchased.*

Outline potential negative consequences

If the other person is still reluctant to agree with what you are asking, you can outline the likely negative consequences for them if they choose not to comply with your wishes. Do not threaten. Simply state what you understand to be the bad things that will happen if things do not change. For example, you could say, "I want you to stop driving past my house. If you continue to drive past, I will seek a legal solution by applying for a restraining order".

It is important to remember that you should only outline negative consequences that you are certain you are willing to follow through on. You, too, have to live with the negative consequences, so do not outline something you are not willing to do or have to happen.

> *If I am prevented from collecting my belongings because you fail to make an arrangement for me or a family member to do so, I will seek the assistance of the police to safely remove my possessions and I will pursue settlement regarding jointly purchased household items.*

So, to summarise, when making a request for change, do the following:

   Define the problem situation

   Describe how you are feeling

   Make your request for change

   Outline possible positive consequences

   Outline potential negative consequences

This is a good approach to standing up for your rights in an assertive manner. It is relatively simple and straightforward. You can also work out in advance what it is you want to say and this protects you from having to make it up on the spot.

However, standing up for your rights may not be enough in itself if you are aiming for assertive communication. You need to be able to negotiate for what you want with a person who may be inclined not to give this to you. This might be any person in your life and not necessarily only your former partner. Consider the following negotiation process.

Negotiating for what you want

To negotiate with another person, your starting point needs to be that you both have needs that are equally important. This will require some effort on your part. It is easy for us to assume that what we want is right and what the other person wants is wrong. However, if you hold this view, then any interaction about the issue in question will be an argument rather than a negotiation.

There are six steps that should be taken when you enter into a negotiation. Let's consider each of these steps.

Know what it is you want

Know what it is that you are negotiating for. You must have a clearly defined goal if you are to enter into a negotiation. If you are not clear about what you want then how can the other person have any idea?

Make a statement of what you want in specific terms

In specific terms and being as clear as possible, make a statement about what you want or do not want to have happen. This can be in terms of what you want or do not want the other person to do. However, it may also be in terms of what you want as the outcome or end goal in other ways, for example, in a property settlement.

Listen to the point of view of the other person

Your aim here is to understand the other person's perspective. To do this, you have to listen carefully to what the other person has to say about their point of view. Rather than just passively listening, you should use active listening skills where you can ask for clarification or elaboration. Remember, you may not agree with the other person's perspective. What you should be doing is appreciating that they have a point of view that might be different from yours, but it is their point of view nonetheless.

Make a proposal

Next, you should make a proposal that offers a resolution. The proposal should not be solely based on what you want. It should take into account the other person's needs. This can be a challenging step that may take some thought on your part. It is easier to conceptualise a proposal that takes into account what both of you want if you approach it with the goal of achieving a 'win-win' outcome. This is where you get some of what you want, and the other person gets some of what they want. A win-win proposal has a much better chance of being accepted than a 'my way or the highway' approach.

Ask for a counterproposal.

If your proposal is not accepted, do not be disheartened. Ask the other person for a counterproposal. Remember that your goal is to reach a point where you can both accept the proposal, even if you both do not get all of what you want.

Aim for compromise

The end result of any negotiation is typically a compromise. You are unlikely to get everything your way, but neither is the other person. You are aiming to reach a middle point that is satisfactory to you both. There are a variety of ways a compromise can be achieved:

> You give up some of what you want to gain some of what you want, and so does the other person.
>
> You might split the difference.
>
> You might agree that you do it your way when you are in control, and the other person does it their way when they are in control.

This last type of compromise can be useful when people cannot agree with parenting rules. In these cases, you might decide that you make the rules when the children are with you, and the other parent makes the rules when the children are with them, as long as the children are safe

Often at the end of a relationship there are issues that will have to be negotiated. You need to feel able to stand up for your rights and you need to be able to negotiate for an acceptable outcome. In doing so, you are aiming for a satisfactory outcome so that you can move on with your life unhindered by unresolved problems.

Improving the quality of your life

Undoubtedly, you are facing a difficult time recovering from the effects of the abuse you experienced and re-establishing your life. You are likely to feel adrift, not only because of the influence of the abuse but because you have disregarded your own needs for an extended period of time.

One thing that can happen as a result of spending a long time accommodating someone else's needs or being focused on surviving is that you lose sight of the things that you can do to please yourself. It is important that you have the opportunity to do some things for yourself. Having a balance between the tasks that are important that you undertake and some leisure time will improve the balance of your life.

It is important that you choose activities that are meaningful to you and that will improve the satisfaction you feel with your life. It is easy to fill your life with things to do, even leisure activities. However, not all of these potential activities will give you a sense of satisfaction. This is because not all activities are important to you. You should choose activities that are of high value to you if your goal is to make your life fuller *and* more meaningful.

How do you know what activities would contribute the most to improving the quality of your life? We often do not think about what we value as we go through our busy day and the question of what a person values can often be confounding to them. Borrowing from a particular therapy called Acceptance and Commitment Therapy, we have included here an exercise in values clarification that will help you decide which activities would be of the greatest value to you.

The goal of this exercise is to identify ways you can put into your life the things that you value the most. The purpose of doing this is to improve your quality of life by having more things in your life that matter to you the most.

When we refer to the things you value, we are not referring to a specific activity. For example, you may have a value related to spending more time with your family. A specific activity that might flow from this value is to have a meal with your family once a week.

Below is a diagram that contains labels for various life domains. A life domain is an area of your life that reflects one portion of who you are and what you do. This is an example of what we are talking about when we refer to your life domain map.

Values clarification exercise for choosing preferred activities

Step 1 involves you listing as many life domains as you can think of that are relevant to you. We have included some life domains that people often list, but feel free to change them and add new ones that reflect your life. What you are doing here is building your life domain map. Take your time to think up as many life domains as you understand to be part of your life. Other examples might be travel, exercise, etc.

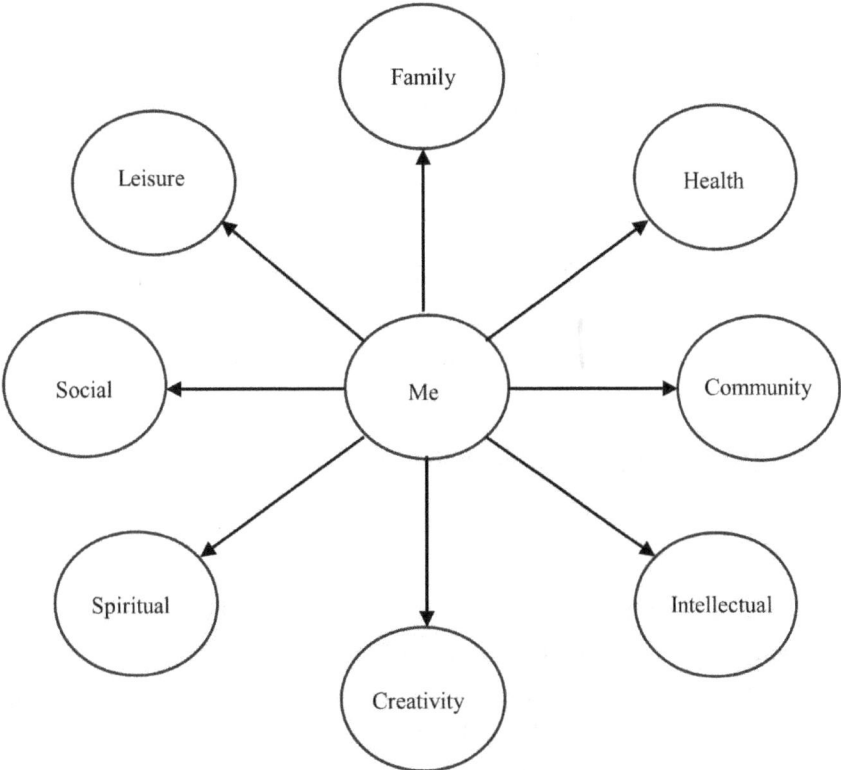

Figure 7: Example of a life domain map.

Step 2 involves you identifying what you already have in your life for the various life domains. Remember, list the values you have (e.g., ample time with your family) rather than specific activities (e.g., Sunday lunch with your family). You will begin to notice that some domains in your life have received lots of attention, but other domains have received little or no attention. Here is an example of the types of values that might appear in the family domain.

> Family domain:
>> Time with family
>>
>> Special time with individual family members
>>
>> Spending time with the young members of my family
>>
>> Important family gatherings

Remember, you are listing here what you already have of value in your life with regard to each domain. This is not a list of the things you would like to have available to you.

Step 3 involves you now considering the things you would like to have in your life in each of the domains. Again, focus on the values (e.g., more quality time with my parents) rather than activities (e.g., visiting my parents on Sunday afternoons).

At this point, you will begin to notice several things.

You will see that there are domains of your life that receive lots of attention already and you want very little else in that domain. Things in these domains are already satisfactory so there is limited purpose in focusing your attention on them.

You will see that there are domains of your life where you have very little, but you also do not really want very much more. These do not deserve your attention either.

Importantly, you will see there are domains of your life where you have very little, and there are many things that you want in that domain that you do not already have available to you. Focusing your attention on these would give you the greatest benefit.

It is the third type of life domain that will become the focus of attention from here on. This is because this focus will have the greatest chance of having the most important impact on the quality of your life.

Step 4 involves focusing on those life domains where you do not have enough of what matters to you, and there is very much more that you want to include in your life. In this step, you should consider how those values that you want to put into your life might translate into specific activities. It is here that the 'what to do' component of the exercise occurs. For example, if you have a value associated with spending more time with your family, you might now consider ways that could happen by identifying specific activities you could engage in that would bring that value into your life (e.g., arranging family get-togethers, organising an online shared family photo site where family members can post photos for all family members to see).

Step 5 involves identifying any barriers that might prevent you from engaging in these activities that would bring the things that you value into your life and finding ways around these barriers. For example, you may not be able to catch up in person with family members if they live in places distant from you, but you could overcome this barrier by arranging online get-togethers.

Of course, there will be things you want that are of value to you that you just cannot have because of real limitations. For example, you may like to travel, but you cannot do so because you cannot afford the expense. However, if travel is of high value, then the quality of your life might be enhanced by spending time exploring places online or watching travel documentaries. Although not exactly what you would give the highest value, these activities are still related to the thing that matters to you.

Remember that your goal is to introduce into your life activities that are of high value to you that will improve the quality of your life. If you are going to devote the time to engaging in these types of activities, it will matter that you focus on the activities that are associated with your highest values.

Some final points

There are a number of points that need to be made or restated.

No one deserves to be abused by an intimate partner. This is true no matter what your former partner told you or led you to believe. Violence towards a partner, in any form, is not an appropriate way for anyone to communicate their needs, express their displeasure or exert control and influence.

The experience of abuse in an intimate relationship can have profound psychological effects. Everyone is vulnerable to these types of effects. Even people who functioned well psychologically before the relationship can still be harmed by intimate partner abuse.

You are not to blame for the behaviour of another person. Your former partner chose to behave the way she did, and you should not take responsibility for her actions.

Many people, probably the majority, have an odd tendency to feel guilty for things over which they genuinely have no control. If you have knowingly done something to harm someone, you should feel guilty. However, it is not appropriate to feel guilt for someone else's choices or behaviour. Choose a different, more accurate emotional response to what has happened. For example, you might feel disappointment that the abuse happened, resentment that you had to go through those experiences, regret that you did not walk away sooner, or even compassion for the abuser because of the problems with which she was obviously burdened. However, do not feel guilt for another person's poor choices and behaviour. All of these alternative and more accurate emotional states are legitimate and are much more manageable psychologically than guilt.

Your future should not be determined by the abuse you experienced. After you leave a relationship, the risk of abuse diminishes, and with every passing day, your abusive experiences increasingly become historical events in your life and not your current circumstance. Dwelling on the 'what if...' and 'if only...' in relation to the abusive relationship just keeps you in a past you have no power to change. Learn to accept what has happened and look forward to a better future. Remember that it is not what happened to you that will determine the future but what you choose to do about the effect on you of the abuse. Choose a better future.

It is possible to have a good future and a new, loving relationship with a different person. Understand that a good quality relationship is characterised by equality and reciprocity and not power-imbalance, control and aggression.

In the aftermath of an abusive relationship, it is easy to believe you would find it impossible to trust anyone and allow yourself to be vulnerable. However, it is worth remembering that trust is earned. All that is required of you is that, when you are ready, you give a person the opportunity to demonstrate to you that they are trustworthy and allow them the chance to act in ways that will earn your trust.

We wish you well for the future.

Additional readings

Eifer, G.H., Forsyth, J.P., & Hayes, S.C. (2005). *Acceptance and commitment therapy for anxiety disorders.* New York: New Harbinger Publications.

Kennerley, H., Kirk, J., & Westbrook, D. (2016). *An introduction to cognitive behaviour therapy: Skills and applications (3rd edn).* London: Sage Publications.

Paterson, R.J. (2023). *The assertiveness workbook: How to express your ideas and stand up for yourself at work and in relationships.* London: New Harbinger Publications.

Sears, R.W. (2021). *The sense of self: Perspectives from science and Zen Buddhism.* Springer Nature.

Tobin, D., Holroyd, K., Reynolds, R., & Wigal, J.K. (1989). The hierarchical structure of the Coping Strategies Inventory. *Cognitive Therapy and Research, 13(4),* 343-361.

www.ingramcontent.com/pod-product-compliance
Lightning Source LLC
Chambersburg PA
CBHW081522160426
43195CB00015B/2472